Conducting Behavioral Consultation in Educational and Treatment Settings

Critical Specialties in Treating Autism and
Other Behavioral Challenges

Series Editor
Jonathan Tarbox
University of Southern California, Los Angeles, CA, United States

Conducting Behavioral Consultation in Educational and Treatment Settings

James K. Luiselli
Melmark New England, Andover, MA, United States, and
William James College, Needham, MA, United States

ACADEMIC PRESS

An imprint of Elsevier

Academic Press is an imprint of Elsevier
125 London Wall, London EC2Y 5AS, United Kingdom
525 B Street, Suite 1800, San Diego, CA 92101-4495, United States
50 Hampshire Street, 5th Floor, Cambridge, MA 02139, United States
The Boulevard, Langford Lane, Kidlington, Oxford OX5 1GB, United Kingdom

Notices
Knowledge and best practice in this field are constantly changing. As new research and experience broaden our
understanding, changes in research methods, professional practices, or medical treatment may become
necessary.

Practitioners and researchers must always rely on their own experience and knowledge in evaluating and using
any information, methods, compounds, or experiments described herein. In using such information or methods
they should be mindful of their own safety and the safety of others, including parties for whom they have a
professional responsibility.

To the fullest extent of the law, neither the Publisher nor the authors, contributors, or editors, assume any
liability for any injury and/or damage to persons or property as a matter of products liability, negligence or
otherwise, or from any use or operation of any methods, products, instructions, or ideas contained in the
material herein.

British Library Cataloguing-in-Publication Data
A catalogue record for this book is available from the British Library

Library of Congress Cataloging-in-Publication Data
A catalog record for this book is available from the Library of Congress

ISBN: 978-0-12-814445-9

For Information on all Academic Press publications
visit our website at https://www.elsevier.com/books-and-journals

Working together
to grow libraries in
developing countries

www.elsevier.com • www.bookaid.org

Publisher: Nikki Levy
Acquisition Editor: Emily Ekle
Editorial Project Manager: Barbara Makinster
Production Project Manager: Priya Kumaraguruparan
Cover Designer: Vicky Pearson Esser

Typeset by MPS Limited, Chennai, India

To my parents, Christine and James,

and to Tracy, Gabrielle, and Thomas,

profound gifts of the past, present, and future

CONTENTS

ABOUT THE AUTHOR

James K. Luiselli is a licensed psychologist, diplomat in cognitive and behavioral psychology (ABPP), board certified` behavior analyst (BCBA-D), and Director of Clinical Development and Research at Melmark New England located in Massachusetts. Dr. Luiselli is the editor, senior editor, and coeditor of 15 books in the areas of clinical psychology, applied behavior analysis, intellectual and developmental disabilities, sport psychology, and performance management. His publication record also includes more than 60 book chapters and 260 journal articles. He has extensive editorial experience, serving as guest editor for eight special-topic journal issues, associate editor for three peer-reviewed journals, and board of editors for ten other peer-reviewed journals.

Series Foreword: Critical Specialities in Treating Autism and Other Behavioral Challenges

PURPOSE

The purpose of this series is to provide treatment manuals that address topics of high importance to practitioners working with individuals with autism spectrum disorders (ASD) and other behavioral challenges. This series offers targeted books that focus on particular clinical problems that have not been sufficiently covered in recent books and manuals. This series includes books that directly address clinical specialties that are simultaneously high prevalence (i.e., every practitioner faces these problems at some point) and yet are also commonly known to be a major challenge, for which most clinicians do not possess sufficient specialized training. The authors of individual books in this series are top-tier experts in their respective specialties.

The books in this series will help solve the problems that practitioners face by taking the very best in practical knowledge from the leading experts in each specialty and making it readily available in a consumable, practical format. The overall goal of this series is to provide useful information that clinicians can immediately put into practice. The primary audience for this series is professionals who work in treatment and education for individuals with ASD and other behavioral challenges.

These professionals include Board Certified Behavior Analysts (BCBAs), Speech and Language Pathologists (SLPs), Licensed Marriage and Family Therapists (LMFTs), school psychologists, and special education teachers. Although not the primary audience for this series, parents and family members of individuals with ASD will find the practical information contained in this series highly useful.

Series Editor
Jonathan Tarbox, PhD, BCBA-D
FirstSteps for Kids
University of Southern California, Los Angeles, CA, United States

Jonathan Tarbox, is the Program Director of the Master of Science in Applied Behavior Analysis program at the University of Southern California, as well as Director of Research at FirstSteps for Kids. Dr. Tarbox is the Editor of the *Journal Behavior Analysis in Practice* and serves on the editorial boards of multiple scientific journals related to autism and behavior analysis. He has published four books on autism treatment and well over 70 peer-reviewed journal articles and chapters in scientific texts. His research focuses on behavioral interventions for teaching complex skills to individuals with autism, treatment of feeding disorders, and the application of Acceptance and Commitment Therapy to applied behavior analysis.

INTRODUCTION

Behavioral consultation is widely recognized as an effective practice for delivering professional services to children and adults in educational and treatment settings. Although different stages and methods of behavioral consultation have been identified (D'Zurilla & Goldfried, 1971; Erchul & Martens, 2010; Kratochwill & Bergan, 1990; Luiselli & Diament, 2002), the fine-points of implementing effective practices are rarely detailed in books and journal articles. For example, what steps does a behavioral consultant take to build a positive relationship with referring agencies? How should a behavioral consultant speak to and interact with service-recipients to gain their acceptance and approval? What practice management skills should a behavioral consultant possess within the larger scope of service delivery?

My path to becoming a consultant began in graduate school when a professor asked if I would be interested in picking up a few hours at a small habilitation setting serving adults with developmental disabilities. He thought I would be able to help the staff there implement behavior support plans and that I would gain some experience delivering consultation. I quickly took to the role of a consultant, made this a focus of my supervision, and sought additional opportunities. Upon completing graduate school, I took steps toward establishing a private practice that combined office and consultation services. Over many years my practice grew until I was eventually spending most of my time consulting to educational, human services, pediatric nursing care, mental health, and forensic settings. Later, I helped establish consultation services at several behavioral healthcare programs while also training and supervising graduate students, psychologists, and behavior analysts in diverse areas of consultation. My work then and now has also included speaking, writing, continuing education, and conducting research pertinent to the professional training and practice of consultation.

Conducting Behavioral Consultation in Educational and Treatment Settings is a practitioner guidebook to implementing consultation with care-providers of children and adults who have learning and behavior challenges. The guidebook focuses on the interactive, problem-solving, dispute resolution, performance management, and related skills necessary for conducting behavioral consultation successfully. The topics are covered in "how to" chapters that feature explicit practice recommendations, strategies for consulting competently, and practice aides in the form of tables, charts, and checklists. Most of the chapters also contain case examples and vignettes which illustrate these skills "in action."

Among several unifying topics in the guidebook, I concentrated on (1) basic principles and practices of behavioral consultation, (2) roles, expectations, and responsibilities of a behavioral consultant, (3) establishing consultation relationships, (4) consulting within problem identification, problem analysis, intervention implementation, and intervention evaluation phases, (5) supervision, (6) interpersonal skills, and (7) performance management. These topics do not exhaust all of the areas subsumed by behavioral consultation but in my experience, they represent requisite competencies for practicing consultation effectively.

Being a practitioner-focused resource, I have deliberately kept the tone of this guidebook nonacademic and free of extensive publication citations. However, where appropriate, I reference the research literature in order to credit the empirical bases of recommended consultation practices. I also provide a brief reference section of seminal, influential, and suggested readings on behavioral consultation.

The educational and treatment settings addressed in the guidebook include public and private schools, residential-care facilities, community-based habilitation centers, group homes, therapeutic day programs, and similar venues. The primary target audience is professionals who provide consultation services, namely board certified behavior analysts, licensed psychologists, school psychologists, counselors, supervising teachers, and behavior support specialists. I also prepared the guidebook as a resource for undergraduate and graduate students, postgraduate trainees, and other individuals seeking specialty training. The guidebook meets the needs of practicing consultants, new practitioners, and students by highlighting the skills that make consulting work effective, and presenting strategies that lead to competent practice.

The guidebook considers behavioral consultation for children and adults who have diagnoses of autism spectrum disorder, intellectual disability, academic learning problems, attention deficit hyperactivity disorder, traumatic brain injury, and other challenging conditions. Admittedly, this is a diverse population with both complementary and disparate clinical priorities. However, there is a rich research literature and body of meaningful practice expertise that supports this widespread application of the principles and procedures of behavioral consultation.

Finally, I have tried to select my words carefully throughout the guidebook, writing in plain English, and avoiding technical jargon, whenever possible (Lindsley, 1991). I use "she" and "he" and "her" and "his" interchangeably, and emphasize person-first language. Because I take the craft of writing seriously, my greatest hope is that what you read is clear, precise, and unambiguous, hopefully contributing to your practice skills and professional development.

CHAPTER 1

Behavioral Consultation: Basic Principles and Practices

Behavioral consultation is generally understood as a model of indirect service delivery (Fig. 1.1) in which the "client" is one or more individuals responsible for program intervention with children and adults. I hereafter refer to the recipients of consultation as "consultees," broadly encompassing teachers, therapists, direct-care staff, counselors, and administrators, among many other service providers. The consultant advises, directs, and many times supervises consultees, thereby providing intervention to children and adults indirectly.

Contemporary behavioral consultation generally follows a multistage model that progresses sequentially through five phases (Kratochwill, Eliot, & Stoiber, 2002) and is detailed extensively in Chapters 3–7. Briefly, the first phase of consultation is *building a consultative relationship* with referral sources and consultees. Next, the consultant moves to the *problem identification* phase in which the goal is to establish consensus about presenting problems, define measurement methods, initiate data-recording, and conduct baseline assessment. In phase 3, *problem analysis*, the consultant works with consultees towards function-based assessment and assessment-derived intervention. With *plan implementation*, consultees apply consultant recommendations while receiving performance-focused supervision and feedback. Lastly, phase 5 entails *plan evaluation* through measurement of intervention effects, collateral behavior-change, and social validity. Though these phases have distinct procedures and objectives, implementing behavioral consultation successfully requires flexibility and creativity. Although the overall framework described in this book is research-proven, implementing the model in each individual case is anything but a manualized approach or rigid adherence to methodology.

Conducting Behavioral Consultation in Educational and Treatment Settings.
DOI: https://doi.org/10.1016/B978-0-12-814445-9.00001-8

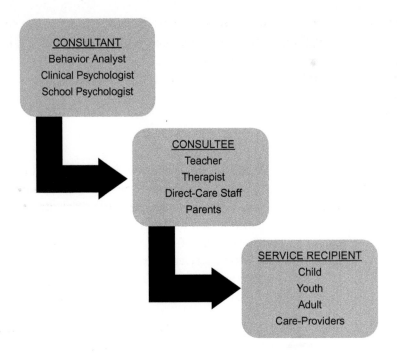

Figure 1.1 Consultation as a model of indirect service delivery.

INTERVENTION FOCUS

Behavioral consultation encompasses three levels of intervention. On a *tertiary level* the concern is instructing consultees in how to intervene with a child or adult who presents with learning and behavior challenges. Using feeding as an example, a focus of tertiary intervention might be a child who displays selective eating, food refusal, or liquid avoidance, which cause the child to be malnourished and underweight. In this example, the child demonstrates a presenting problem, with clear negative outcomes, and requires systematic intervention.

Secondary intervention is not directed at an existing learning or behavior challenge but instead an existing condition that places a child or adult at-risk for developing a problem. With feeding, an example would be a child who displays a tendency toward preferential eating or a parent who mismanages meals. Effective consultation in such cases would target these risk factors through prevention-focused intervention.

Finally, the emphasis of *primary intervention* is preventing the emergence of risk factors. Using the feeding example again, the concern for consultation might be training parents and care-providers to select nutritionally sound food choices and use positive approaches to making mealtimes enjoyable, apply procedures that support a child's self-feeding, and implement antecedent strategies which deter the child from acquiring disruptive mealtime behaviors.

VOLUNTARY PARTICIPATION

Consultation services work best when consultees independently seek and voluntarily participate in the services provided by the consultant. Voluntary engagement with a consultant suggests that consultees are motivated to gain advice, without constraint, and with anticipated positive results. Of course, in the real world of consultation practice, we routinely confront consultees who do not desire to listen to recommendations or join with a process that may have been mandated by a program administrator. DiGennaro Reed and Jenkins (2013) also pointed out that due to legislative regulations such as the Individuals with Disabilities Education Improvement Act (IDEIA, 2014), "consultation is no longer considered a voluntary activity and educators have less flexibility to reject or decline assistance" (p. 320). The simple fact is that not every consultee is going to greet a consultant with open arms or demonstrate the enthusiasm that accompanies voluntary participation. Later chapters in the guidebook suggest consultation practices for building receptive relationships with consultees.

[handwritten margin note: AX from schools?]

COLLABORATIVE PROBLEM-SOLVING

Problem-solving is the foundation of behavioral consultation and necessitates fluid collaboration between consultant and consultees. Some of the terms that describe collaborative problem-solving are "shared responsibilities" derived from "mutual decision-making" that reflects "respect" among participants and in a "nonhierarchal arrangement." Like virtually all of the practices described in this guidebook, collaboration is established when a consultant behaves strategically in gaining the appeal and approval of consultees.

Being respectful means that a consultant recognizes the critical role consultees play in delivering services within educational and treatment settings. At the start of consultation services, I always defer to consultees as the "local experts"—they are better informed about, have

[handwritten note: ↑ Nice!]

interacted more frequently with, and know the presenting problems of children and adults well beyond my knowledge base. Taking the time to listen to consultees unconditionally and with dedicated purpose establishes the respect which so fundamentally forms the basis of productive consultant–consultee relationships.

One additional point of emphasis is that the objectives of consultation should be driven by consultees. From the onset of delivering services, the consultant should make clear that her/his essential role is to respond to the needs of consultees. The consultant will typically help clarify and refine consultation objectives, but the direction should be forged by the individuals who are principally responsible for interacting with children and adults.

PERSONAL MOTIVATION

Do we do this with grphomes?

The personal motivations of consultants and consultees are notably similar for wanting to help and improve quality of life of children and adults and build exemplary services at educational and treatment settings. Other motivations are distinctly different, not inherently bad or even unexpected, but points of view that must be reconciled with the real contingencies governing practice. My somewhat tongue-in-cheek perspective is that consultants want to (1) have their recommendations followed precisely, (2) be admired by consultees, and (3) demonstrate success to the people who hired them. Consultees have different motivations, namely to (1) gain respect from the consultant, (2) be told how to fix the problem, and (3) avoid more work as much as possible. While this caricature is an oversimplification and meant to be humorous, it helps us all remember that we are human and that both consultees and consultants are *always* affected by multiple sources of motivation, some more helpful and some less. Think of acknowledging similar and different motivations, points of reference, and desires of consultants and consultees as having the same beneficial effect of assessing the preferences of a child, adult, and care-provider before initiating a person-specific intervention or systems-level plan.

Two other motivations guide consultation practice. First, at a most basic level, consultants are trying to sell a product. Our commodity is expertise in understanding and changing behavior of the individuals who educate, treat, and support children and adults, operate human services programs, make decisions about professional training, and write policies affecting standards of care. Whether a consultant is focused on one teacher interacting with a single student, organizational change at a residential treatment facility, or supervision of care-providers, the invariant challenge is convincing consultees to adopt methods that are often unfamiliar to them, perceived incorrectly, and viewed with apprehension. Having knowledge about what to do is by itself insufficient unless a consultant can persuade consultees to behave differently, in effect, "buy" what we are selling.

The second motivational factor is that consultants strive to achieve a gold standard of implementation practice, and rightfully so. We want consultees to understand the conceptual bases of our procedural recommendations and faithfully perform activities such as conducting preference assessments, recording data without omissions, and applying extinction for challenging behavior with fidelity. In delivering consultation, we desire to perform as we were trained, bringing behavior analysis expertise to every situation, and rigorously adhering to evidence-supported methodologies. Unfortunately, consulting is a messy job and does not readily conform to best practices, even those contained in this guidebook! The demands and constraints of most educational and treatment settings frequently require consultants to reassess their objectives and interactions with consultees. We should not expect, for example, that public school teachers will be familiar with schedules of reinforcement, that parents will grasp principles of behavioral momentum, or residential care-providers will have experience with transfer-of-stimulus control interventions. Nor should we assume that purportedly well-trained practitioners within ABA programs will be fully competent in applying routine procedures. I believe that one key to consultation success is recognizing when and how to adjust our gold standard expectations without sacrificing professional acumen and sophistication. Without qualification, we should tediously seek perfection while realizing and humbly accepting that the work with consultees may not achieve our most lofty goals.

CHAPTER SUMMARY

- Behavioral consultation follows a multistage model that begins with building a consultative relationship.

- Behavioral consultation encompasses tertiary, secondary, and primary intervention.
- Effective-problem solving is a key competency for working with consultees.
- Understanding the motivations of consultees will inform consultation practices.

CHAPTER 2

Roles, Responsibilities, and Expectations of a Behavioral Consultant

Most educational and treatment settings have "internal" professional staff who function in a consultative capacity. If you are a psychologist, behavior analyst, or hold a similar position you likely carry a clinical caseload, contribute to treatment teams, consult with families, and evaluate intervention plans. In-house consultants typically have a position title (e.g., Director of Behavioral Services), administrative responsibilities, access to diverse setting resources, and regular salary with associated benefits like health insurance, retirement account, and sick time.

Employment at an educational or treatment setting may be part- or full-time. Having a set schedule, defined responsibilities, and secure salary are some of the advantages of delivering consultation services as a setting employee. Conversely, there may be constraints that impede practice options and administrative-organizational conundrums that cannot be overcome. For example, several years ago I delivered a presentation that was titled, "Organizational Incompetence: What's a Behavior Analyst to Do?" The presentation described many "macrolevel" impediments I had encountered as a psychologist responsible for numerous consultation activities at several behavioral healthcare settings. One setting in particular resisted evidence-based applications of organizational behavior management performance improvement tactics, instituted inequitable policies among staff, and engaged in behaviors that conflicted with the *Professional and Ethical Compliance Code for Behavior Analysts* (Behavior Analyst Certification Board, 2016). In my presentation I discussed the pressures and profound malaise the setting had created for me and many colleagues, our carefully planned efforts to resolve the problems, and the limited success we had. At another setting, the executive leadership made unilateral and impulsive decisions, ignored input from "lower-ranking" professional staff, and communicated so poorly that practice initiatives were

Conducting Behavioral Consultation in Educational and Treatment Settings.
DOI: https://doi.org/10.1016/B978-0-12-814445-9.00002-X

frequently thwarted. Be aware of these organizational roadblocks and how they can compromise your consultation capacity.

By contrast, consultants "external" to educational and treatment settings operate independently through a solo or group practice. In this capacity, they establish service contracts that specify the content of consultation, number of contact hours per week—month, performance expectations, and monetary fees. Independent status enables consultants to operate with greater flexibility and autonomy but the picture is not as rosy at it may seem. Thus, a consultant in private practice has to generate referrals, deal with fluctuating service fees, pay special attention to business demands (billing, office help, accounts payable and receivable), and produce billable units. And in private practice, there are no sick days and paid vacation time!

As noted, consultants assume many roles with consultees, advising about individual children and adults, evaluating systems issues that impact programs, training care-providers, conducting supervision, and organizing performance improvement projects. Regardless of purpose or objectives, most consultants will implement several common procedures.

REVIEW OF RECORDS AND FILE DOCUMENTS

As a first step in delivering consultation, it is desirable to review as many records and file documents that are available. This information describes history and pertinent details in the form of reports, case notes, correspondence, test results, assessment protocols, and sometimes documents prepared by previous consultants. I try to arrange and read records-file documents in chronological order, looking for similarities and discrepancies among them, usually highlighting notable text passages, and writing notes on a summary form.

OBSERVATIONS

Best practices in consultation frequently entail direct observation early on. If you are retained as a consultant to develop a behavior support plan for a child at school, you will schedule one or more classroom observations. Delivering consultation services with parents requires observing a child at home. If the intent of consultation is to design a training series for direct-care providers, they will have to be observed interacting with the people they serve. During observations, consultants take notes, record data, fill out forms, and/or follow a structured instrument that organizes key indicators. Direct observation gives the consultant a first-person account of natural conditions in which children, adults, and consultees interact. When observing, consultants need to be cautious of reactivity effects on the persons being observed and not creating situations that might alter the normal course of events.

INTERVIEWS

Interviews with consultees allow them to voice their concerns and respond to inquiries from the consultant. It is useful to schedule interviews following a review of records-file documents and conducting observations because the consultant can pose clarifying questions, ask for additional information, and correct any misinterpretations. The content of interviews is largely determined by the focus of consultation. For example, the interview format when completing a functional behavioral assessment might include administration of indirect assessment checklists and rating scales such as the *Motivation Assessment Scale* (*MAS*) (Durand & Crimmins, 1988), *Functional Assessment Screening Tool* (*FAST*) (Iwata, DeLeon, & Roscoe, 2013), and *Questions About Behavior Function* (*QABF*) (Paclawskyj, Matson, Rush, Smalls, & Vollmer, 2000). More open-ended interviews let a consultant transition to and from various topics depending on the responses of consultees. Whenever possible it is always desirable to interview multiple consultees individually and compare the judgements of these informants.

PREPARING WRITTEN DOCUMENTS

Consultants prepare many written documents such as progress notes, assessments, proposals, instructional guidelines, behavior support plans, and many other similar products. These documents are most helpful when they are prepared and submitted in a timely manner and accurately describe the conduct and outcomes from consultation. Some written documents may be one-time products, for example, an assessment report, whereas progress notes, meeting summaries, and data entries are usually prepared periodically throughout the course of ongoing consultation. Fig. 2.1 depicts a simple *Consultation Case Note* for summarizing activities and recommendations from a consultation contact. The consultant records the date of service, identifies the consultation activities that were conducted, writes a brief description of the consultation, and lists recommendations. The completed consultation case note is given to consultees immediately following each contact or can be emailed at a later date.

Consultation Contact
Date of Service:
Child-Adult:
School-Agency:
Consultation Activities
[ ]   Observation [ ]   Review of records-data [ ]   Consultee meeting [ ]   Other meeting [ ]   Preparation of documents-materials [ ]   Other activities:
Consultation Description
Consultation Recommendations
1:
2:
3:
4:
5:
Consultant signature:
Date of next consultation:

Figure 2.1 Consultation case note.

CORRESPONDENCE

Though the bulk of consultation takes place on-site at educational and treatment settings, ongoing correspondence between consultant and consultees is required between visits. These contacts occur as telephone calls, text messages, and emails, are vital for maintaining communication, and serve multiple functions such as updating progress, troubleshooting, confirming appointments, and deciding about interim recommendations. The relative ease of contemporary electronic communications adds greatly to consultation efficiency.

MONITORING SERVICES

Consultants must monitor the time spent reviewing records-file documents, conducting observations, interviewing consultees, preparing written products, and corresponding. These process measures ensure accountability of service delivery and provide a quantified record of activities. I also find that carefully monitoring services is a good source of feedback that provides useful information about my own performance, allowing me to see how much time I devote to consultation, whether I am practicing good performance management skills, and what, if any, factors impede efficiency.

Needless to say, most consultees look to consultants as a source of expert advice. Three of the most impactful contributions to exemplary practice are a consultant's (1) technical knowledge, (2) experiences with service delivery, and (3) self-awareness of practice boundaries. The *Professional and Ethical Compliance Code for Behavior Analysts* (Behavior Analyst Certification Board, 2016) is explicit with regard to fundamental practice guidelines:

- "Behavior analysts rely on scientifically and professionally derived knowledge when making scientific or professional judgments in human service provision..." (p. 4).
- "Behavior analysts provide services, teach, and conduct research only within the boundaries of their competence, based on their education, training, supervised experience, and appropriate professional experience..." (p. 4).
- "Behavior analysts who engage in assessment, therapy, teaching, research, organizational consulting, or other professional activities maintain a reasonable level of awareness of current scientific and professional information..." (p. 5).

Recognizing your knowledge base, experiences, and scope of competencies should be a continuous process of self-assessment that dictates your consultation activities. It would be tempting, for example, to consult about behavior support intervention with a child who has attention deficit hyperactivity disorder (ADHD) but only if you are educated about ADHD symptomatology, *DSM-V* diagnostic criteria, executive functioning, learning disabilities, and psychopharmacology. If requested to consult with a program for persons with traumatic brain injury, you need to be familiar with neuropsychological testing, post-injury sequelae, and models of rehabilitative care.

The following activities are effective strategies for professional self-assessment and continuous process improvement:

CONSTRUCT A DEDICATED PROGRAM OF CONTINUING EDUCATION

This component of professional development will be directed by the continuing education (CE) requirements of licensing and credentialing boards (American Psychological Association, Behavior Analyst Certification Board, National Association of School Psychologists) which prescribe the minimum number of CE hours required within yearly and multiyear cycles. As you accumulate CE credits, try to select topics that advance your knowledge beyond the familiar domains of ABA and behavioral psychology. Many times, new topics will emerge as your consultation practice expands into less familiar areas and especially within multidisciplinary educational and treatment settings. Realize, too, that some CE pursuits may not provide approved credits by your particular credentialing agencies. Nonetheless, you should consider any CE activities that will contribute to your professional growth as a consultant.

My own development as a consultant illustrates the wide lens to adopt in using CE to foster consultation practice. At one time I was contracted to provide behavioral consultation to a specialized child and adolescent inpatient unit at a psychiatric hospital. The hospital offered numerous multidisciplinary CE events I was able to attend and on topics that were germane to my work on the unit: diagnostic formulation, substance use, major mental illness, and psychopharmacology. I had training in some of these and related areas but in other areas, no training or related clinical experiences. I found these CE events greatly improved my performance as a consultant, enabled me to practice more effectively among multidisciplinary professionals, and built a foundation for further advancing my skills with similar patient populations.

CE was also instrumental in my development as a consultant to attorneys engaged in litigation cases. I started by conducting independent educational evaluations of students receiving special education services and disputes that arose between schools and families concerning the contents of individualized education programs, curricula, resource allocation, and placement decisions. As this work continued I found it necessary to attend legal workshops and seminars aimed at psychologists, counselors, and other behavioral healthcare professionals. Through CE, I gained greater knowledge about testifying in court and litigation hearings, writing evaluation reports within the legal arena, rules of order (discovery, attorney–client privilege, admission of evidence), and related competencies. I eventually evolved my consultation practice to include specialty work with attorneys, broadening my involvement and CE to forensic and malpractice cases.

MAKE A PLAN TO STAY CURRENT WITH THE PROFESSIONAL LITERATURE

It bears repeating that staying current with the professional literature is necessary for practicing competently and in most cases credentialing organizations emphasize this activity as another facet of CE. Reading and reviewing books, chapters, and journal articles occurs routinely as undergraduate and graduate students but not uncommonly, diminishes in the face of practice demands. I recommend several steps that Mattson (2017) advised practitioners to follow for reading the professional literature:

Schedule time each week for dedicated reading. Plan for reading articles much the same as you would plan program meetings, supervision sessions, parent conferences, or any related activity that forms consultation practice.

Set performance objectives. Be explicit about your goals, for example, identifying and reading one journal article per week that relates to a consultation case you are working on.

Become efficient at identifying and obtaining copies of journal articles. Take some time and intentionally practice until fluency with the process of accessing the professional literature via search engines and electronic data bases. If necessary, science librarians should be consulted and publisher email alerts can be set up to learn the most recent articles contained in a vast array of journals. In particular, if you are a BCBA but do not work at a university, make frequent use of the free access to journal articles that is available through the Behavior Analyst Certification Board's web portal.

Journal clubs make it possible for practitioners to meet, review publications, and provide yet another option for staying current with the professional literature (Parsons & Reid, 2011). Participants can select topics of mutual interest, each person agreeing to summarize one or more sections of an article, then report to the group. A journal club or similar forum offers social support to individuals who may find it difficult setting up and adhering to an individualized reading plan. The varied perspectives of club readers is another advantage of a group format. If the organization housing the journal club is a provider of BACB CE units, meetings can be designed to also provide CEs, a further incentive for practitioners to attend the meetings.

CONFER WITH COLLEAGUES

Conferring with colleagues is routinely advanced as a critical element of professional development. These associations are often prompted when, as consultants, we encounter a particularly challenging situation that can benefit from the view of an independent and objective set of eyes. But meeting with colleagues on a regular basis outside of high priority cases and projects is also meaningful. At various points in my career I sought out other consultants and we planned group contacts several times per year to share experiences and discuss matters that applied to our practices. If you are on staff at an educational and treatment setting it should be relatively easy to assemble colleagues for similar purposes.

Like other guidelines for professional development, you should document the frequency and content of collegial conferences. Keep track of your deliberations and decisions, particularly if you discuss sensitive topics that apply to consultees, service recipients, and administrative-organizational exigencies of service settings. Such records do not have to be extensive but should summarize how your interactions with colleagues informed practice. As always, be mindful of HIPPA and FERPA regulations any time you discuss case details with professionals outside of your practice or service setting.

CHAPTER SUMMARY

- Consultants operate as independent practitioners and in-house personnel at educational and treatment settings.
- Essential activities that consultants perform include reviewing records-file documents, conducting observations, interviewing consultees, preparing written documents, maintaining correspondence, and monitoring services.
- Practice skills and competencies are strongly dependent on a consultant's technical knowledge, experiences with service delivery, and self-awareness of performance boundaries.
- Meaningful self-assessment can be accomplished by constructing a program of continuing education, staying current with the professional literature, and conferring with colleagues.

CHAPTER 3

Establishing a Consultation Relationship

This initial phase of consultation sets the tone for delivering services effectively with consultees. Among many factors, consider that in most cases consultants and consultees have never met each other, individuals may perceive the process of consultation differently, personal and professional biases are present, language and communication abilities vary, and everyone likely has different expectations. At this beginning stage, consultees will attend to your physical appearance, verbal expression, social graces, and the like before thinking about the hard issues that will be addressed through consultation. As the consultant you will be sizing up the people in the room, how they react to your words, whether they appear knowledgeable, and what kind of impression you make. Suffice it to say, the consultant–consultee relationship typically starts with uncertainty and needs thoughtful focus from day one.

RESPONDING TO REFERRALS

One situation that will not initiate a successful consultation relationship is accepting referrals which are beyond your level of competency or based on limited or misunderstood information. Too often, consultants take on service requests without clarifying the details because they are urgently seeking or are excited about the prospects of new business. Other practitioners with consultation responsibilities may be uncomfortable with a referral but think they have to respond unconditionally. For example, many early-career behavior analysts employed at educational and treatment settings encounter consultation demands from administrators that are unrealistic and poorly conceived. I have had these experiences and witnessed the same among both junior and senior colleagues. For further discussion on this matter, readers may wish to reference *Practical Ethics for Effective Treatment of Autism Spectrum Disorder*, by Brodhead, Quigley, and Cox (2018).

Conducting Behavioral Consultation in Educational and Treatment Settings.
DOI: https://doi.org/10.1016/B978-0-12-814445-9.00003-1

Fig. 3.1 is a sample form for documenting referrals and the general information needed to make a decision about services. This type of form is most relevant for independent consultants in a solo or group practice. Notice that an initial referral record does not have to be overly complicated but instead, a concise document that identifies the origin, purpose, and pragmatics of a consultation request. With such information, you can properly judge whether the referral is unreasonable or does not fit with your areas of expertise. If you decline a referral, you can suggest other consultants to the referral source. Should you be comfortable with the initial referral, there will be more conversation

Referral Contact
Date of referral:
Received by:
Referral source:
Telephone:
Fax:
Email:

Referral Request

Service Fee Information
Rate quoted:
Billing source:
Contract administrator:

Action Plans
1:
2:
3:
4:
5:

Figure 3.1 Initial referral record.

and correspondence before consultation begins, including but not limited to (1) acquiring records-file documents, (2) obtaining signed release of information forms, (3) preparing a services contract, and (4) having the services contract approved and signed by the responsible parties.

What about receiving a questionable referral or request for consultation in your role as a behavior analyst, psychologist, or clinician within an educational and treatment setting? In such cases, I suggest speaking with the person(s) who made the referral and explaining your concerns. Matters of competency can be addressed by citing guidelines of responsible professional conduct applicable to your discipline. You being able to confidently respond to a referral may also entail proposing additional assessments, medical screening, more resources, or consideration of alternative placement. Support from colleagues can also greatly assist your advocacy in this regard.

EXPLAINING PURPOSES AND OBJECTIVES OF CONSULTATION

Most consultees are not involved in recruiting and hiring a consultant, may be uninformed or misinformed about the purpose of consultation, and know nothing about the consultant's background and expertise. The consultant—consultee relationship will be facilitated by taking time to review key elements of the consultation process. Such information sharing usually occurs during an initial meeting with consultees. The following are some guidelines for doing this effectively:

Tell consultees how you were hired and how the referral of concern came your way. For example, if you have been brought in to a public school to consult on a student or to a classroom, specify who initially contacted you (e.g., Director of Student Services, Administrator for Special Education), the arrangement of services, your understanding of the issues at hand, and other similar matters. If your position is within an educational and treatment setting, clarify the origin of your involvement in a similar way, even if you think consultees have this information or are familiar with your role.

Discuss your role as consultant with them. It is important to begin the consultant—consultee relationship with consensus among all of the participants. Be open to questions and any inquiries that clarify your work. And be exacting in your answers, down to the number of hours you will be on site and days—weeks—months of anticipated service.

Allow time for consultees to introduce themselves. In addition to introductions, ask consultees to describe their position in the educational and treatment setting. Again, you will be familiar with some of these individuals if you function as an internal consultant. For new consultees it is imperative that you learn about their general activities and specific involvement in working with you as consultant. Intentionally making time to hear from the consultees about their job also serves the function of showing respect and building rapport with them.

Briefly present your background and credentials but do not overdo it. Most consultees are not interested in the colleges or universities you attended, your graduate training, how many certifications you have, or a recitation of your presentations and publications. Many teachers, for example, have had plenty of experience with "experts" who have fancy degrees and titles but not the slightest idea about what it is like to be in the classroom. A more effective approach is to simply tell consultees how your background relates to the consultation issues being discussed. The simple rule of thumb is to act with humility and deference towards the local experts from the beginning and through all phases of the consultant−consultee relationship.

Summarize the process and next steps. When you perceive that introductions and exchanges of information have been properly addressed, begin talking with consultees about the next steps of consultation, which could be scheduling observation, acquiring records-file documents, assigning tasks, or conferring with other individuals. At this point in the process consultees and the consultant should be fully appraised of and agree with a preliminary action plan.

Concluding. Before ending the initial meeting with consultees, distribute your contact information (address, cell phone, email) in the form of a business card or one-page details sheet. Emphasize that you welcome and encourage communication between consultation visits.

ASSESSING INTERVENTION PHILOSOPHY

Consulting to an educational and treatment setting that adheres to an ABA orientation will be different from consulting to a program that primarily adopts a different perspective. At the heart of this matter is learning everything you can about the setting's intervention philosophy, the types of procedures that are approved for implementation, current instructional-treatment plans, and mission statement. Settings you are accustomed to make this process a lot easier compared to novel environments and with consultees who have not yet benefited from substantial ABA training.

Becoming familiar with a setting's intervention philosophy allows you to plan consultation activities strategically, such as the language you use with consultees, explanation of learning principles, instruction in data recording, and numerous implementation guidelines. Multidisciplinary settings comprised of special education teachers, occupational therapists, psychiatric nurses, social workers, and paraprofessional staff must be thoroughly evaluated so that you can judge their receptivity to behavioral consultation. Other concerns that behavioral consultants should consider when assessing the intervention philosophy of interdisciplinary settings are (1) identifying opportunities to promote ABA, (2) ethical obligations to propose alternatives to nonbehavioral methods, and (3) applying a decision-making model to address questionable educational-treatment recommendations (Brodhead, 2015).

WHO IS IN CHARGE?

Independent consultants to educational and treatment settings are "outsiders" without administrative authority over staff. Even in-house practitioners may be restricted in their managerial decision-making. The operational hierarchy of settings can vary considerably, therefore understanding who is in charge and behaving accordingly are instrumental to consultation success.

In illustration, within public elementary, middle, and high schools, the buck usually stops at the principal's office. Principals are intimately involved with all aspects of school climate, school district policies, hiring practices, teacher supervision, distribution of resources, and so on. How does the principal and her/his administrative team typically deal with these and related responsibilities? Does the principal like to see things in writing before rendering decisions? How does the principal conduct meetings with staff, is she/he a task master, or more often than not delegates action plans to subordinate personnel? These are just some of the questions to ask in guiding your school consultation practice.

Your consultation activities at other educational and treatment settings, whether as an internal or external practitioner, should be similarly focused by addressing the question, Who is in charge? Most human services programs will have an administrative hierarchy comprised of clinical directors and supervisors. The structure of a residential treatment facility typically includes a program director, assistant director, and family services specialist. All, some, or none of these individuals may be tied to your work as a consultant so take time to learn about their roles, performance expectations, quirks, relative strengths and weaknesses, and perceptions about you!

The basic operational components of an educational and treatment setting may be as simple as always signing in at a main office when you arrive, calling specific individuals to schedule appointments, wearing a "visitor's pass" when on premises, signing out records-file documents, and adhering to a dress code. If you ignore these and similar conventions, you run the risk of highlighting your status as an outsider. Be perceptive about setting expectations and adapt your behavior accordingly.

PREVIOUS EXPERIENCE WITH CONSULTANTS

In an earlier section of the guidebook I discussed the importance of explaining your role as a consultant to consultees. Consistent with this level of information sharing, ask consultees about their prior experiences with consultants. Some individuals may have never interacted with a consultant or only had fleeting contacts. Other consultees may report one or more negative encounters with consultants, which you should try to explore: what were the circumstances associated with these experiences, were they one-time events or repeated with other consultants, how did the consultations end? For example, in many schools and organizations, teachers and staff are highly accustomed to being exposed to a new "flavor of the week" consultation each year or each time administrative leadership changes. Indeed, in such situations, employees have often learned to exert minimal effort and simply wait until events pass, thereby enacting no meaningful change. Actively seeking out existing perceptions of consultees will allow you to sort out attitudes and perspectives that can guide your consultation services toward more favorable outcomes.

At the same time, find out from consultees what they liked about prior consultations. Their opinions may have to do with personal characteristics of consultants, the demands that were placed on consultees, details about communication, and particular interpersonal skills. If you know what the consultees you are working with liked about other consultants, you can then adopt those behaviors and evaluate whether your performance has similar effects. This assessment of social validity is examined more fully in Chapter 7, Consultation in Action: Intervention Evaluation.

ESTABLISHING RAPPORT

The impetus for establishing rapport with consultees, indeed the foundation of this guidebook, is contained in the following quote from Gutkin and Curtis (1982): "At its most basic level, consultation is an interpersonal exchange—the consultant's success is going to hinge largely on his or her communication and relationship skills" (p. 822). A later chapter in the guidebook is devoted exclusively to these skills and how they influence building rapport with consultees.

Rapport, broadly defined, encompasses likeability among individuals, consistently pleasant exchanges, mutual positive regard, empathy, and harmony. Colloquial descriptions of rapport would be that people "get along with each other" and they have "good chemistry." More behavior-specific indices of rapport would concentrate on operationally defined verbal and nonverbal behaviors such as language content, eye-contact, and body posture.

The importance of building rapport among consultant and consultees is heightened at the initial stage of establishing a consultation relationship. To reiterate, there is the novelty of the situation, expectations of the participants, previous experiences with consultation, and people simply getting to know one another. Research into the association between rapport and relationship formation informs us that as consultants we should carefully monitor consultees, assessing their interests, beliefs, values, and goals. With reference to Chapter 9, Likeability, Performance Management, and Conflict Resolution, we should strive to find common ground with consultees, allowing them to see you as reasonable, inclusive, and tolerant. I think of establishing rapport as *successive approximation* whereby a consultant shapes commonality with consultees, gradually advancing dialogue in different directions as such conditions arise, but not posing challenges at a level that could harm the positive relationship that was formed.

Being aware of and sensitive to diversity and cultural facets among consultees is another prerequisite to building rapport and supporting success within all stages of consultation. Important and distinguishable differences apply to race, ethnicity, religion, socioeconomic status, gender identity, age, and nationality. A person's self-identify, group affiliations, and strength of cultural values must not be overlooked.

Below are a few examples of how diversity and culture can impact consultation services, interactions with consultees, formulating intervention plans, and performing outcome evaluation. Each example centers on home-based consultation with families and their child with developmental disabilities.

Child A presents with eating problems related to self-feeding, food selectivity, and disruptive behavior during meals. Within his family's culture, people customarily eat with their hands and share food portions from the same containers at meals.

Child B sleeps erratically, usually getting up between 2:00—3:00am, and climbing into his parents' bed, where he remains until wake-up in the morning. His family reports that within their culture, young children often sleep with their parents and they do not object to this practice.

Child C lives with an extended family comprised of her parents, siblings, aunts, and grandparents. In this family's culture multiple family members take responsibility for childcare and assume the role of parent-surrogate.

The preceding examples illustrate the complexity of implementing consultation with individuals whose customs, values, and world views may differ from our own. A consultant in these cases would have to evaluate the extent to which the practices in each family might deleteriously affect intervention recommendations or whether family members would even consider changing their approaches to the children. There may be language barriers that make communication difficult, reactions that are driven by perceived authority, misinterpretation of nonverbal behaviors, and other social nuances that set the occasion for uncomfortable interactions. To improve consultation practice, Fong,

Catagnus, Brodhead, Quigley, and Field (2016) posited that "it is important to be aware of one's own biases or preconceived notions as a behavior analyst, as well acknowledging limitations on one's cultural knowledge" (p. 86). As you build diversity and cultural sensitivity towards consultees, continue your self-assessment, confer with mentors and colleagues, and adopt a nonjudgmental perspective when listening to and conversing with consultees. Actively prompt yourself to practice perspective taking. For example, ask yourself questions such as, "Even though I don't agree with their values and beliefs, if *I was coming from that perspective*, how would I view the recommendations I am trying to convince them of?" or "Is there any other way to get my point across that might be more valid when viewed from their cultural perspective?"

CHAPTER SUMMARY

- Establishing a satisfying consultation relationship begins by responding properly to consultation requests and referrals.
- Ensure that consultees clearly understand the purposes and objectives of consultation.
- Assess the intervention philosophy of educational and treatment settings.
- Understand the administrative and operational hierarchy of educational and treatment settings by asking and answering the question, who is in charge?
- Ask consultees to describe their previous experiences with consultants.
- Concentrate on establishing rapport with consultees by honing your communication and relationship skills.
- Be sensitive to and educate yourself about matters of diversity and unique cultural perspectives.

CHAPTER 4

Consultation in Action: Problem Identification

At this phase of consultation, you will have conducted an initial meeting with consultees, possibly a second meeting, at which time introductions were made and participants discussed the goals, focus, and general procedures of consultation. In the problem identification phase, the consultant and consultees should establish a regular meeting schedule that can be followed with fidelity. Finding a mutually accommodating meeting schedule is not a simple task but necessary in order to provide consultation effectively. The following considerations apply to the schedule and content of meetings.

Who comprises the consultation team? Not everyone who attended the preliminary meeting will be actively involved with consultation. For example, administrative personnel at an educational and treatment setting may be present initially to hear about a plan for consultation but not be responsible for implementing recommendations. The actual consultees are more likely to be teachers, therapists, residential staff, and other direct-care providers. These individuals should comprise a team, organized by the consultant, that will be present at scheduled meetings. The more definitive the team, the better able the consultant will be to coordinate and monitor service delivery.

When are consultees available for meetings? Consultees have varied responsibilities but almost always are extraordinarily busy, with little idle time. Productive meetings with consultees are only possible if they can assemble on days and times that accommodate their work schedules. Of course, a consultant also has schedule constraints—however, she/he should defer to the demands placed on consultees, not the other way around.

Have consultees review their weekly schedules as a first step towards confirming meeting dates and times. Be aware of conflicts that may prevent consultees from attending meetings such as late-afternoon family commitments, union employee restrictions, other meetings requiring attendance, and competing activities. I have

Conducting Behavioral Consultation in Educational and Treatment Settings.
DOI: https://doi.org/10.1016/B978-0-12-814445-9.00004-3

found it necessary to arrange meetings with consultees at the start of the school day before students arrive, during lunch breaks, and at special times in the day when other staff had to "cover" for meeting participants. It is worth the extra effort to build a meeting schedule that ensures full attendance rather than having limited participation because consultees must be elsewhere.

Monitor attendance. Tracking attendance at meetings can be accomplished by having consultees sign in each time they assemble with the consultant. Explain to consultees that the meeting sign-in makes everyone accountable for routine attendance and joining fully in consultation deliberations. If attendance wanes among some consultees, you are able to contact them individually to clarify expectations and troubleshoot any difficulties with scheduling. This process represents good performance feedback that is so essential throughout consultation.

Prepare an agenda. Meetings run more smoothly when there is a written agenda. The agenda should capture the most current and critical topics under discussion and fit with the scheduled duration of the meeting. Fig. 4.1 is a type of meeting agenda form that can be used at the problem identification phase of consultation and other phases as well. The form lists the key points to be addressed in the meeting, areas of discussion, and recommended action plans. I advise sending a written agenda to consultees several days preceding a scheduled meeting so that they can prepare. Also, the type of meeting agenda form shown in Fig. 4.1 can be distributed later to consultees as a brief summary document. Before a meeting adjourns, have consultees contribute to planning the next agenda.

Meeting basics. Much has been written about the "art and science" of conducting meetings. First and foremost, a meeting leader sets the tone for conduct and decorum. Your consultation skills must include modeling the behaviors you want to see demonstrated by consultees during meetings: arriving on time, following the agenda, patiently conversing and listening to each other, responding respectfully to differing views, and staying focused on the central topics. Furthermore, a meeting leader is principally responsible for keeping discussions on point, managing time, summarizing decisions, and setting action plans. Concerning time, meetings that exceed 60 minutes are usually unproductive so it is best to keep between 30 and 45 minutes in order to maintain attention among consultees and respect their schedules.

Meeting date:
Meeting participants:

Agenda Items
Problem Identification:
Key discussion points:
Recommended action plans: 1: 2: 3: 4: 5:
Consultant signature:
Date of next meeting:

Figure 4.1 Meeting agenda form—problem identification.

RESOLVE DISCREPANCIES

One of the first steps in problem identification is resolving any discrepancies among consultees concerning consultation targets and objectives. This emphasis underscores the common theme of promoting consensus among members of the consultation team. As examples, if consultation is directed at a student attending a public or private school, is the presenting problem completing academic tasks, reducing instruction-interfering behaviors, or a combination of both? If the reason for consultation is training residential-care staff to record program evaluation data, how many data sources will be selected. With home-based consultation for a child who sleeps poorly, will parents be intervening to overcome bedtime resistance, early morning wakening, or daytime napping?

My experiences have taught me that many complications with consultation result because insufficient time was spent with consultees making sure they agreed on identified problems. Fig. 4.2 is a checklist that includes several critical indicators to be reviewed with consultees

Date:
Child-Adult:
School-Agency:
Checklist Items
1: Definition of presenting problem:
2: Occurrence indicators (check and describe): [ ] high frequency [ ] long duration [ ] high intensity [ ] low frequency-high intensity [ ] other:
3: Negative outcomes (check and describe): [ ] self-harm [ ] harm to other people [ ] environmental disruption-destruction [ ] socially stigmatizing [ ] compromises instruction [ ] other:
4: Setting factors (check and describe): [ ] school-service setting [ ] home [ ] work [ ] community [ ] other:
5: Intervention history:

Figure 4.2 Problem identification checklist for children–adults.

in reaching consensus and resolving discrepancies about presenting problems of children and adults. A similar checklist can be designed when the objective of consultation is to resolve systems-level and large-scale performance concerns. This format can be useful because it identifies several characteristics of presenting problems, including risk factors, that may otherwise be overlooked at the early stage of consultation.

The problem-solving foundation of behavioral consultation is ideally suited to shaping identification-consensus among consultees. One option is asking consultees to independently prepare written definitions of presenting problems, which can then be compared and contrasted through consultant-led discussion. This activity is a good start towards ongoing collaboration that is necessary between the consultant and consultees. By identifying and defining problems objectively, consultees also learn how to function as an empirical practitioner.

REVIEWING RELEVANT INFORMATION

The consultant should have access to all relevant files, records, and reports that are pertinent to the consultation referral. It is desirable to review this information before the first problem identification meeting. A records-file documents review should give an historical perspective on the presenting problems, detailing previous problem definitions, intervention objectives, and outcome data. Not all prior documents will contain this information but any confirming or disconfirming evidence will be of value. Be sure to inquire about documents that may be referenced but are not included in your review of files. Also, not all records and files will be found in a single source so you may have to locate documents in several locations.

MEASUREMENT

When problem identification is completed, the next task should be preparing a measurement protocol. Behavior analysts are well aware that measurement choices will depend on the number and topographies of target responses, intervention objectives, contextual variables, and evaluation strategies. For skill acquisition targets, the measurement opportunities can range from quantity of correct trials, percent accuracy, frequency or rate of adaptive behaviors, and permanent products, to name a few. Behavior reduction targets encompass frequency, duration, time-sampling, and interval recording methods. Consultants must carefully appraise consultee experience with measurement and data-recording before designing a protocol. Furthermore, I find it necessary to emphasize three fundamental measurement priorities in order to achieve "buy in" from consultees:

1. Measurement is needed to properly evaluate the effectiveness of interventions that consultees implement.
2. Measurement begins before intervention in order to determine a baseline level of presenting problems.
3. Measurement continues throughout intervention to judge the progression of effects and revise procedures accordingly.

The consultant should take full responsibility for selecting a measurement protocol, in collaboration with consultees. Although it is possible to choose a standardized instrument, I recommend designing one or more "homegrown" protocols that can be tailored to the unique features of each consultation case. Discussions with consultees will help clarify the ideal measurement method, conditions, and data-recording forms. The approach to measurement should be driven by practical considerations. For example, will the protocol adequately document the identified problems while also requiring low response effort and ensuring acceptable reliability? Other considerations are whether consultees will perform measurement using pencil-and-paper or automated data-tracking devices, how recorded data are to be summarized and archived, and which on-site consultee is tasked with coordinating these activities.

Fig. 4.3 illustrates a measurement protocol I designed with colleagues in a systems-level consultation project to improve the appearance, organization, and safety of special education classrooms (Schmidt, Urban, Luiselli, White, & Harrington, 2013). The three domains included in the *Classroom Ecology Checklist* (General Classroom Arrangement, Classroom Appearance, Safety Hazards) were derived from several meetings with classroom teachers, who were the consultees, and school supervisors, who implemented a teacher training intervention. The supervisors completed the checklist during two daily 5-minute observations conducted in four classrooms by recording whether each within-domain measure was achieved, not achieved, or not applicable. This measurement method was deemed to be most

Classroom:	
Observer:	Primary [ ] IOA [ ]
Date:	
Time:	

Scoring Key: 0 = NOT ACHIEVED 1 = ACHIEVED   NA = NOT APPLICABLE

A. General Classroom Arrangement	
1. Teacher's desk free of food containers, paper refuse, stacked objects	0 1 NA
2. Teacher's work station free of food containers, paper refuse, stacked objects	0 1 NA
3. All posted information is stapled (not tacked) to a bulletin board: no paper taped or tacked to walls	0 1 NA
4. Instructional materials are in storage areas/cabinets/shelves when not in use: not left on tables or chairs	0 1 NA
5. Program books/data clipboards are in storage areas/cabinets/shelves when not in use: not left on tables or chairs	0 1 NA
PERCENT ACHIEVED	

B. Classroom Appearance	
1. Student belongings (backpacks, coats, footwear, lunch boxes) are in cubbies/closets	0 1 NA
2. Staff belongings are in closet	0 1 NA
3. Chairs (any portion) are under desks/tables with legs on the floor unless being used for activity or instruction	0 1 NA
4. Edible items are in closed containers	0 1 NA
5. Information Center includes only required postings as per reference diagram	0 1 NA
PERCENT ACHIEVED	

C. Safety Hazards	
1. Classroom is free of obvious hazards (e.g., exposed wires, hanging shelves, or broken windows)	0 1 NA
2. Tables are free of food and liquid debris	0 1 NA
3. Floor is free of food and liquid debris	0 1 NA
4. There is non-obstructed pathway to all fire exits	0 1 NA
5. Sharp objects (scissors, knives, tacks, forks) are not in the environment	0 1 NA
6. Cleaning supplies/toxic substances (sanitizers, cleaning fluids and wipes) are not in environment	0 1 NA
7. Objects are not on top of "high rise" cabinets	0 1 NA
8. Keys are not in classroom or cabinet doors	0 1 NA
9. Furniture is stable and in good repair	0 1 NA
10. Closet and cabinet doors are closed	0 1 NA
PERCENT ACHIEVED	

COMPOSITE CLASSROOM RATING
(Total Number of 1 Ratings/Total Number of 0+1Ratings)

Figure 4.3 Classroom ecology checklist (CEC).

applicable to the project because the teachers were not able to record data contemporaneously with their other duties. The supervisors found it easy to integrate measurement into their already existing schedules and the data proved to be sensitive to intervention changes.

ESTABLISHING A PRECONSULTATION BASELINE

There are several ways to approach baseline assessment with consultees. In some cases, measurement may already be in place and the consultant can review these data to determine if the information is acceptable or warrants revision. One illustration would be staff at a day-treatment setting who are recording frequency of challenging behaviors among several children or adults. However, on close inspection it is revealed that their data-recording is inconsistent and only reflects certain periods in the day. Or, residential-care providers may be completing data-recording forms retrospectively at the conclusion of their scheduled shifts and not in real time. The consultant in these situations would need to advise consultees about revising their recording practices so that data reflect an accurate baseline.

Consultees at other education and treatment settings may be unfamiliar with measurement methods and have to be persuaded to engage in baseline assessment. Some consultees question the need for such assessment, concluding that they already know enough about the problems, or questioning the rationale for establishing a baseline. I always inform consultees that knowing objectively what the level of "distress" is before consultation gets started is a prerequisite for supporting and justifying their efforts towards intervention success. A simple example, displayed in Fig. 4.4, is a plot of the percent of learning objectives in a student's IEP that teachers worked on each week. These data, if recorded during a preconsultation baseline phase, reveal a performance percent that must be improved. Helping consultees to initiate the data-recording of completed IEP objectives produces a relatively simple but valid measure for evaluating teacher-directed consultation recommendations.

CHAPTER SUMMARY

• Schedule, plan, and conduct effective meetings with consultees.

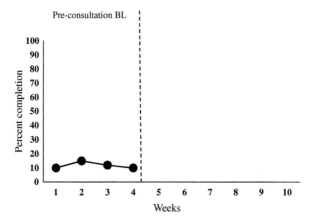

Figure 4.4 Measurement example.

- Resolve discrepancies among consultees at the beginning phase of problem identification.
- Review and document all relevant information pertinent to consultation objectives.
- Design measurement methods that consultees can implement efficiently and accurately.
- Have consultees conduct preconsultation baseline assessment.

CHAPTER 5

Consultation in Action: Problem Analysis

The problem analysis phase of consultation is largely devoted to functional behavioral assessment (FBA) and answering questions about the interpersonal, environmental, and organizational influences on presenting problems. For children and adults, different indirect and descriptive FBA methods are available, there are many resources that describe the assessment process (Call, Scheithauer, & Mevers, 2017; Neidert, Rooker, Bayles, & Miller, 2013), and most behavior analysts are well trained and experienced with FBA implementation. Similar assessment is also possible in organizational-focused consultation. For example, the *Performance Diagnostic Checklist* (*PDC*) (Austin, 2000) is a 20-item questionnaire that is administered to managers and supervisors within business and industry settings to assess antecedents and information, equipment and processes, knowledge and skills, and consequences that contribute to poor performance of employees. A variant of the *PDC*, the *PDC-Human Services* (*PDC-HS*), can be used to functionally assess variables associated with performance strengths and weaknesses of care-providers at educational and treatment settings (Carr, Wilder, Majdalany, Mathisen, & Strain, 2013).

The findings from FBA and other initial assessment activities inform intervention and consultation recommendations. Written plans should be prepared in the form of easily understood procedural guidelines. Most commonly, these formats include behavior support plans, instructional protocols, intervention checklists, project policies-procedures, and implementation handbooks which will be formulated from ongoing consultant–consultee meetings. In this context, the consultant (1) trains consultees to conduct functional assessment, (2) interprets assessment findings, (3) recommends intervention strategies, and (4) prepares the written documents.

Below are practical tips for creating excellent written documents in the context of consulation.

Conducting Behavioral Consultation in Educational and Treatment Settings.
DOI: https://doi.org/10.1016/B978-0-12-814445-9.00005-5

An Objective Record. A written description of intervention procedures gives consultees an objective record of how procedures should be applied. Without such documentation, procedures are likely to be implemented arbitrarily and with poor intervention integrity.

Be Concise. Written procedural documents do not have to be excessively long. Keep the documents as brief as possible so that consultees will refer to and not ignore them.

Avoid Jargon. Avoid using technical language, unnecessary jargon, and "behaviorese." For example, instead of writing, "Implement social extinction when Bill verbalizes a profane word," have the statement read, "Do not look at or speak to Bill when he verbalizes any of the following words --------."

Write for the 3rd Grade Reading Level. There is empirical evidence that the text contained in behavior support plans and related documents should be written at a 3rd–4th grade reading level. Some consultees may be challenged by the written word and have difficulty comprehending cumbersome text passages. Keep to basic language that consultees can understand.

Get a Second Set of Eyes. Have one or more people without a human services background read your written documents before distributing them to consultees. If they can accurately describe the procedures, you are on the road to clarity.

Aim for First-Time Comprehension. A simple rule of composition is writing sentences that can be understood the first time someone reads them (I hope the preceding sentence qualifies!).

Include Revision Dates. Written procedural documents are frequently revised on an ongoing basis—be sure to indicate the dates of revision and when modified procedures take effect.

In summary, consultants should prepare written plans and intervention guidelines to maximize comprehension by consultees. Do not expect that consultees will embrace a 17-page behavior support plan (I have seen them!), follow such a plan as written, or be able to explain the plan correctly to other care-providers. Certainly, written documents that describe procedures must be conceptually sound, assessment-informed, and function-based, but not at the expense of confusing the very people charged with implementing those procedures. If you want to develop a good self-monitoring habit, use the bulleted list of tips above as a checklist each time you prepare a written consultation document and do not turn in the document to consultees until you have considered each tip.

TRAINING REQUIREMENTS

Are consultees sufficiently skilled to implement your consultation recommendations? This is one of several questions that should be posed during problem analysis and intervention formulation. Direct questioning of consultees is a face valid approach that can be pursued during individual or group meetings. So, if you are consulting to educators about discrete trial teaching (DTT) with students, you can ask about their general knowledge, understanding, and experiences with such instruction. This background information will dictate the training methods that are most applicable.

Didactic Training. This approach to training is similar to a classroom presentation or lecture. The consultant assembles consultees, explains concepts and procedures, gives illustrations, and supplements training with reading materials or possible video depictions. As per the preceding example, the content of training would include basic principles, research support, and common applications of DTT. Time during training should be set aside for group discussion and clarification with consultees.

Didactic training is a good first step with consultees who have limited knowledge and experience in the areas to be addressed through consultation. The training is relatively noninvasive, easy to conduct, and time-efficient. Unfortunately, what consultees learn with didactic training rarely transfers to actual performance. Knowledge gained is always desirable but consultation training inevitably has to move on to building competencies and skills.

Simulated Training. Through simulated training, the consultant instructs consultees under conditions that mimic natural situations at educational and treatment settings. In such training, a consultant might arrange a space with desks, chairs, and materials that resemble the location for DTT in a classroom. Apropos to training in simulation, a consultee would assume the role of a child or adult, the consultant demonstrates how DTT should be implemented, and each consultee follows the demonstrated behaviors. The consultant coaches consultees by delivering instructions, prompting responses, and presenting feedback through praise and correction. There is repeated practice throughout training until consultees reach a mastery performance criterion which suggests they can be observed outside of simulated sessions.

The benefit of simulated training is having consultees experience and practice the behaviors needed to interact effectively with children and adults. I emphasize that such training also applies to other consultation objectives. For example, a consultant may be involved in teaching consultees best practices for conducting parent training, supervising careproviders, writing reports, or themselves learning to train other individuals. Simulated training that progresses from didactic instruction, to modeling, to role-play with feedback until mastery criteria are met, is often referred to as behavioral skills training (BST) and is supported by extensive research (Parsons, Rollyson, & Reid, 2013). Note however, that despite the evidence supporting BST, skills do not always generalize to working with children and adults in educational and treatment settings so in vivo training is often required as well.

In Vivo Training. When applying in vivo training, a consultant works directly with consultees under natural conditions. These interactions may follow one or more sessions of simulated training or start fresh without extensive preparation. However, the training procedures used by the consultant are as described previously: instructions, demonstration, prompting, and performance feedback. In vivo training is ideal because it takes place in the environments where children and adults receive services. This arrangement is highly desirable for teaching and maintaining competencies of consultees.

As applied to DTT, Gilligan, Luiselli, and Pace (2007) conducted in vivo training with three teachers at a school for children with developmental disabilities. We prepared a 10-step DTT checklist to document their demonstration of instructional responses with students during baseline and training phases. A consultant trained the teachers by (1) having them read a written protocol for implementing DTT, (2) observing teaching sessions, (3) praising steps in the DTT checklist the teachers executed accurately, and (4) correcting misapplied steps with brief practice. This in vivo training was performed "on the spot," in each teacher's classroom, lasting 5−8 minutes per consultant−consultee interaction. The training was rapidly successful in boosting performance of DTT to near-100% accuracy with the three teachers.

RESOURCE REQUIREMENTS

Consultants need to assess the resources consultees require to carry out recommendations. Begin with *people resources* by asking if there are sufficient staff to manage programs, record data, attend meetings, and so on. I have witnessed many consultations where personnel shortages hampered my ability to provide adequate services or make reasonable suggestions. Not infrequently, these circumstances demand attention from senior authorities at educational and treatment settings. In effect, the consultant may have to inform decision makers about limited staff resources and the impact on consultation services. I have seen the matter arise when schools could not add support for classroom teachers, project improvement teams were improperly constituted, and inpatient units were unable to guarantee adequate numbers of staff on assigned shifts. Difficulties with people resources are perhaps the most pressing concern for consultants working into the problem analysis phase.

An additional area that must be further assessed are *material resources*, which includes everything that consultees need on a day-to-day basis. Are there paper, clipboards, markers, and folders for recording and summarizing data? What are the computer and information technology resources at the educational and treatment setting? Consultants must also inquire about materials that may be needed for data recording, such as tally counters, timers, and affordable software/applications. Various objects and activities will have to be obtained as reinforcers prescribed in intervention plans and performance projects— are they readily available, have to be purchased, or possibly need to be procured from other sources? Not wanting to appear oddly compulsive, I advise taking an inventory of material resources available to consultees relative to a "wish list" that is based on consultation recommendations.

CONSULTEE ACCEPTABILITY

Throughout the consultation process, consider what consultees think about your recommendations and their willingness to implement them. This type of social validity assessment is reviewed in depth in Chapter 7, Consultation in Action: Intervention Evaluation, as a component of intervention evaluation but is also pertinent at the problem analysis phase. For example, Durand (2008) described an approach toward preintervention assessment with families of children who have ASD and sleep problems. The *Selecting Sleep Interventions Questionnaire (SSIQ)* asks parents to rate (Yes/No) their tolerance to bedtime disruption by their child, willingness to change sleep schedules, and perceived barriers to intervention success. The questionnaire is intended to tease out procedures that families are reluctant to implement and to clarify attitudes about intervening with their child. The results from the *SSIQ* are incorporated for tailoring interventions to the unique circumstances of each family as opposed to making recommendations that are unappealing and unlikely to be applied with fidelity.

Consultants can adapt a similar strategy with consultees. The form shown in Fig. 5.1 is a way to preview intervention recommendations

Consultation Information		
Date of Service:		
Child-Adult:		
School-Agency:		
Meeting Attendance:		
Assessment Information		
Assessment Questions	YES	NO
Do you approve of the intervention objectives?		
Do intervention recommendations seem appropriate for presenting problem(s)?		
Do you suggest changing any of the intervention recommendations?		
Do you require additional resources to implement intervention recommendations?		
Do you anticipate any barriers to implementing intervention recommendations?		
Assessment-Derived Action Plans		
1:		
2:		
3:		
4:		
5:		

Figure 5.1 Problem Analysis Acceptability Assessment.

by posing questions to consultees and recording their suggestions. This acceptability assessment functions as a risk−benefit evaluation of intervention objectives and recommendations, conducted in group meetings, and promoting meaningful input from consultees. As noted in earlier chapters, having consultees contribute in this way demonstrates respect for their opinions, which reinforces a problem-solving orientation, builds solidarity among consultation team members, and validates problem analysis decisions. At this level of consultant−consultee collaboration, one or more assessment-derived action plans can be proposed and, if approved, completed before intervention implementation.

CHAPTER SUMMARY

- Prepare brief, concise, and easily understood written documents.
- Assess training needs of consultees.
- Combine didactic, simulated (behavioral skills training), and in vivo training methods.
- Identify people and material resources needed to comply with consultation recommendations.
- Evaluate consultee acceptability of consultation objectives and recommendations.

CHAPTER 6

Consultation in Action: Intervention Implementation

At the intervention implementation phase, consultants continue to train consultees with respect to recommendations and initial written documents. By this time the consultant and consultees will have participated in several meetings and reached consensus about consultation objectives, specific procedures, data recording, and high priority concerns. With regard to training, a consultant's leading activities with consultees will encompass three primary domains: (1) observation, (2) intervention integrity assessment, and (3) performance feedback. These activities have interrelated functions and purposes, most notably in conducting in vivo training and supporting procedural fidelity.

OBSERVATION

Most consultees are keenly aware of being observed by a consultant. They worry about not performing skillfully and possibly being criticized for poor judgement or failing to follow recommendations accurately. Observation-induced distress among consultees should be anticipated even with dedicated efforts towards building rapport, positive relationships, and collaboration.

Planned observations of consultees are usually dictated by a consultant's schedule at educational and treatment settings. When scheduling observations, check with consultees to confirm acceptable dates and times. Although some consultants have told me that they occasionally perform unannounced observations, I do not recommend showing up to observe without advanced notification and approval.

Establishing and confirming a schedule will have the added benefit of including and informing all people expected to be present during observations. For example, teachers, teacher-aides, special discipline therapists, and school volunteers may be in a classroom at the same time a consultant is observing. Similarly, in addition to the assigned

Conducting Behavioral Consultation in Educational and Treatment Settings.
DOI: https://doi.org/10.1016/B978-0-12-814445-9.00006-7

shift care-providers at a community-based group home, other people on-site could be a residential program director, nurse, or parents visiting their daughter or son. Make it a point to know your audience beyond the consultees to be observed.

A second critical step is previewing the content of observation with consultees. Providing information about observation to consultees beforehand tends to reduce any preobservation jitters and sets the occasion for a positive experience. I would add that preparing consultees is a simple social gesture that demonstrates respect and will strengthen an evolving relationship with the consultant. The details of observation include the time involved, setting locations, focused activities, and desired outcomes. A consultant should propose these elements of observation and also ascertain the goals and desires of consultees.

During some observations, a consultant will "shadow" consultees, attending to interactions with children and adults that were previously highlighted. The consultant maintains general observation notes but just as often documents specific consultee activities. These observations can be contrasted to more directed training encounters between consultant and consultees. In such situations, the consultant actively engages with consultees through instruction, demonstration, cuing, and other teaching methods consistent with in vivo training.

Observation time should be planned exclusively for consultees without distraction or interruption. Thus, a consultant should not be responding to emails, taking telephone calls, or managing tasks which are not pertinent to observation. Absent an emergency or crisis event, demonstrate to consultees that they have your undivided interest and attention. Similarly, consultants should be careful not to engage in excessive "small talk" with consultees. Some individuals may wish to develop friendly relationships with the consultant and though building rapport is important, nonessential conversations are unprofessional and occupy precious time needed for improving program quality and outcomes.

INTERVENTION INTEGRITY ASSESSMENT

One of the most productive observation objectives for a consultant is assessing intervention integrity of the plans, guidelines, and procedural documents that were developed with consultees. Intervention integrity asks, "Do consultees implement written recommendations accurately?" Also referred to as procedural fidelity, intervention integrity is a critical determinant of program evaluation, has been carefully studied through decades of ABA research, and yielded several empirically supported conclusions.

First, exemplary intervention integrity is achieved when consultees apply procedures with 100% accuracy. Second, a high level of intervention integrity is associated with optimal learning outcomes among children and adults. Said another way, instructional and behavior support interventions are most effective when consultees apply procedures correctly, at all times, with little to no deviation. Third, consults can and should use performance enhancing strategies to improve less than desirable intervention integrity.

Assessment of intervention integrity is mandatory for evaluating consultation practices and recommendations. Picture a consultation project in which consultees at a residential treatment unit are being trained to implement a token economy program with youth who have skills deficits and challenging behaviors. The procedures within the token economy involve prompting daily living and self-care routines, and reinforcing task compliance, following unit rules, and nonoccurrence of challenging behaviors. An initial period of data recording reveals that the program is not highly effective and may have to be terminated. Without assessing intervention integrity, it is not possible to judge whether program ineffectiveness was due to the token economy procedures themselves or misapplication of the procedures by consultees.

A starting point when addressing intervention integrity is recognizing factors that can compromise fidelity. At a minimum, consultants should be aware that implementation by consultees will suffer if intervention plans and guidelines are too complex and demanding. Complexity is evident when consultees have to apply multiple procedures, the procedures are time-intensive, or the conditions for implementation are ill defined. Consultants should also evaluate whether intervention integrity is negatively affected by competing activities that consultees may face. Consultees who were not trained to acceptable performance criteria may further account for integrity problems.

Factors influencing poor intervention integrity can be identified by performing routine assessment during scheduled observations. Each observation is structured so that a consultant can objectively document whether consultees follow procedures accurately according to a checklist that aligns with the written plans and guidelines they are expected to implement. For example, the *Intervention Integrity Assessment Checklist* presented in Fig. 6.1 illustrates a 10-step behavior support plan that was designed to improve a student's transition compliance through a combination of antecedent and consequence procedures. While observing consultees implementing the plan, a consultant records their performance by scoring (1) steps that were implemented correctly, (2) steps that were implemented incorrectly, and (3) steps that were not implemented because the student did not display

Date of Assessment:

Setting:

Student:

Consultee:

Consultant Observer:

Behavior Support Plan Component	Behavior Support Plan Procedures	C (+)	IC (−)	NA
ANTECEDENT	States transition cue ("In two minutes….")			
	Sets interval timer			
	When timer sounds, states, "All done, walk to…." next destination			
	Presents transitional object			
CONSEQUENCE	Praises compliance every 30 seconds			
	If aggression occurs, blocks responses and withholds attention			
	If floor-dropping occurs, moves five steps away, waits for independent standing, resumes transition			
	At destination: Requests transition object			
	At destination: Delivers praise and token			
	Records transition data			

Scoring Key

C = Implemented step correctly
IC = Implemented step incorrectly
NA = Not applicable (no opportunity to respond)

Intervention Integrity Score (correct steps/total steps × 100)

Figure 6.1 Intervention Integrity Assessment Form.

behaviors that were to be followed by specific consequences. Step-by-step analysis produces an overall integrity measure (% of steps implemented correctly) and a breakdown of the exact steps with integrity errors. Multiple observations will confirm where consultees need assistance to bring their intervention integrity scores to an acceptable level.

Instructional protocols in the form of task analyzed sequences and behavior support plans lend themselves to conventional intervention integrity assessment but there are many other applications. I once consulted to an injury reduction program at a residential facility in which care-providers were trained to complete detailed incident reports of injuries they sustained during clinical intervention with children and youth (Luiselli, 2013). The incident reports were tuned to setting-activity variables associated with aggression-produced injuries and these data informed the selection of prevention and physical management procedures. We assessed the integrity of incident reporting throughout the project to ensure that care-providers accurately recorded the necessary data, thoroughly filled out each report, and submitted finalized reports to a designated project manager.

Previously, I concluded that the best outcomes with children and adults occur when consultees implement procedures with 100% intervention integrity. There are some recent research findings suggesting that this standard may not apply in all cases. For example, occasional inconsistent application of "benign" procedures such as differential reinforcement and verbal instructions may not deleteriously affect intervention. Nonetheless, striving for the highest level of intervention integrity represents best practice and there is no substitute for this consultation objective.

PERFORMANCE FEEDBACK

Upon completing observation and assessing intervention integrity, a consultant is able to deliver performance feedback. The feedback focuses consultees on their general actions during observation and specific responses contained in an intervention integrity checklist. The goals of performance feedback are two-fold: (1) to reinforce accurate implementation by consultees, and (2) to correct implementation that is not accurate. I describe below several guidelines for delivering performance feedback most effectively.

Feedback should be as rapid as possible. It is best to present performance feedback to consultees immediately following observation when events are fresh and learning will not be compromised by the passage of time. Accordingly, the consultant and consultee should plan the postobservation performance feedback session in advance and not assume that the necessary time will be available. Some consultees may have to move on to other activities immediately following observation unless their schedules can be adjusted to confer with the consultant. Notwithstanding the advantage of immediate feedback from the consultant, scheduling constraints with consultees may dictate an "end-of-the-day" session that can be conducted faithfully and without interruption.

Provide feedback one-to-one whenever possible. There are occasions where more than one consultee is present to receive performance feedback. This arrangement might be in order when a consultant has to observe multiple consultees interacting simultaneously with children and adults or several consultees are responsible for plan implementation with a single person. However, in most situations a performance feedback session between a consultant and one consultee is preferred. First, many consultees are uncomfortable receiving performance feedback in the company of peers. Individualized attention from a consultant removes group tension and can focus on the individualized training needs of the consultee. At the same time, in a one-to-one format a consultant does not have to shift her/his attention among multiple consultees who inevitably present with different skills. Finally, assembling groups of consultees for the same performance feedback session may be impractical at most educational and treatment settings.

Consider the format of your feedback. Whether delivered to an individual or groups of consultees, a consultant should be attuned to the manner of presenting performance feedback. As the typical format relies on verbal feedback during face-to-face encounters, consultants should consider a consultee's communication skills and tendencies, reactions to observational comments, and responsiveness within a training context. Think of consultant–consultee performance feedback sessions the same way you would conduct FBA: How does your verbal and nonverbal behavior facilitate attention from the consultee, contribute to meaningful conversation, promote understanding, encourage inquiry, and reinforce learning? For some consultees, written feedback may be received better, while others might prefer oral feedback. In summary, know and apply the contingencies that operate productively with every consultee.

Feeback should be specific. Begin the performance feedback session with a brief review of the preceding observation and then refer the consultee to the intervention integrity checklist starting with steps that she/he implemented accurately. Have the consultee follow along with a copy of the checklist. "You presented the reinforcer exactly as described in step 6," and "Well done, you correctly prepared all of the instructional materials," are examples of specific descriptive praise statements a consultant should deliver.

Corrective feedback should be constructive. Correction of steps on the intervention integrity checklist that the consultee did not implement accurately entails (1) identifying each misapplication, (2) describing the expected performance criterion, (3) modeling error-steps correctly, and (4) allowing the consultee to practice proper implementation. The consultant should correct and practice with the consultee in a style that is supportive and instructive, and with positive language that is intended to teach skills and not punish mistakes. The strategy I recommend is, "Here is how to do it, let's practice to get better, that's it, you got it!"

Supplement verbal feedback with graphs. Whenever possible, prepare simple graphs and tables of performance data to review with consultees. One of the easiest effective feedback tools is a figure showing the percentage of intervention integrity steps a consultee performed accurately over the course of consecutive observations. Graphic feedback can be integrated within consultant–consultee sessions or sent via email. For example, in consulting with clinical supervisors at a residential treatment setting (Luiselli, 2009), I identified an objective of increasing their frequency of weekly supervisory observations within assigned classrooms. Several performance monitoring and group review meetings were effective but one of the clinicians required additional email performance feedback (graphs, reminders, performance-contingent praise) to achieve desired results.

Give feedback in frequent brief sessions. Research has shown that performance feedback sessions can be effective at durations lasting no more than 5–10 min. Reduced session length will be well received by most consultees and accommodate schedules at educational and treatment settings.

Conclude feedback sessions with goals to improve performance. Fig. 6.1 also contains space for a consultant to summarize what was addressed during the performance feedback session, planned objectives, and scheduled date for the next observation. Make a copy of the completed form and give it to the consultee when you conclude.

CHAPTER SUMMARY

• Involve consultees and related care-providers when planning and scheduling observations.
• Preview the format and objectives of observations with consultees.
• Eliminate distractions to and interruptions during observations.
• Design observations to assess intervention integrity.
• Individualize the methods, style, and content of delivering performance feedback with each consultee.

CHAPTER 7

Consultation in Action: Intervention Evaluation

Intervention evaluation is dedicated to questions about consultation effectiveness. This process actually begins with a consultant advising consultees early on that measurement and data-recording are key components of service delivery. As intervention evolves in response to consultant recommendations, training, and feedback, consultees are able to see the value of objective measurement that originated at the baseline (preconsultation) phase.

The evaluative measures that resonate most with consultees are the direct effects and outcomes that were selected as primary consultation objectives. Evaluation will want to show that as a result of intervention, skills improved, problem behaviors occurred less frequently, procedural fidelity was better, and quality indicators were affected positively, to name only a few desirable findings.

There are three additional evaluation considerations beyond the essential outcome measures. First, single-case designs enable consultants to assess the control exerted by intervention plans. Second, social-validity assessment, touched upon earlier, expands evaluation to include the perceptions of consultees about intervention satisfaction and acceptability. Third, maintenance evaluation looks at the durability of intervention effects and whether additional procedures are required to support behavior-change long-term. The remainder of this chapter is dedicated to giving practical guidance on how to address all three.

SINGLE-CASE DESIGNS

Single-case designs are synonymous with ABA research but should also be integrated with routine clinical practice. Performing as a scientist−practitioner demands that we evaluate the effects of our practices with the most control and rigor as possible. Single-case designs meet this standard, are adaptable to many consultation projects, and

Conducting Behavioral Consultation in Educational and Treatment Settings.
DOI: https://doi.org/10.1016/B978-0-12-814445-9.00007-9

provide a solid empirical base for the recommendations made to consultees.

Selecting a single-case design depends on factors such as consultation objectives, targeted behaviors, personnel resources, time availability, and exigencies within an educational and treatment setting. Certain designs, described below, will be best applied to skill acquisition measures, while other designs are more suited to behavior reduction interventions. I emphasize that single-case designs are not reserved only for single-person evaluations but have utility with groups of individuals and large-scale systems projects. Nonbehavioral interventions, which will be encountered in multidisciplinary settings, can also be evaluated using single-case designs. I suggest that consultants incorporate single-case methodology in whatever ways are most feasible and will contribute to intervention evaluation.

Consultants should acquaint themselves with single-case designs, terminology, and methods by reading several seminal and noteworthy texts (Barlow, Nock, & Hersen, 2009; Kazdin, 2011). In what follows, I describe the essential features of four single-case designs that consultants can implement in their practice. These are very brief descriptions and do not exhaust the many alternatives and adaptations that are available.

Reversal (A-B-A-B) Design. The hallmark of this design is conducting an initial baseline phase (A) and then introducing (B), removing (A), and reimplementing intervention (B). Control is revealed when behavior "reverses" during phase changes. Variants of the A-B-A-B reversal design include different combinations of intervention procedures that are systematically introduced and withdrawn. For example, a two-component intervention could be evaluated in an A-BC-A-BC sequence or an intervention withdrawal analysis in an A-BC-A-BC-B-A-B format.

It is not easy asking consultees to stop applying a seemingly effective intervention plan in order to conduct a reversal evaluation. Further, such evaluation is contraindicated when the goal of intervention is to eliminate self-harming, aggressive, destructive, and similar high-risk behaviors. Rather, consider an A-B-A-B reversal design for evaluating instructional plans, environmental modifications, and non-complex interventions that (a) can be quickly introduced, removed, and introduced again, (b) are likely to produce reversible effects, and (c) consultees will not resist. Examples in a classroom would be evaluating the presence and absence of an assistive technology device, cuing procedure, strategic seating arrangement, or stimulus presentation on student learning. A systems project might entail adding and removing elements of a personnel training program or performance improvement initiatives. These and similar evaluations frequently do not require extended reversal-to-baseline phases, thereby limiting the time needed to confirm intervention outcomes. If the reversal effect is immediate, sometimes only one or two data points will be required to clearly make the case that interventon was responsible for behavior change and should remain in place.

Multiple Baseline Design. Multiple baseline designs are relevant for many problems and situations referred to consultants. The multiple baseline across behaviors design is indicated when a child or adult presents with two or more skill acquisition or behavior reduction objectives. General clinical practice finds that one intervention target is usually the rule and not the exception. Recording data for several measures will naturally fit with implementation of a multiple baseline across behaviors design and sequential introduction of intervention with each measure.

A multiple baseline across settings design allows a consultant to evaluate intervention plans with children and adults who present similarly within two or more locations. Relevant illustrations for consultants would be a child who has been referred for consultation at school and home, and an adult who requires services at a vocational training program and residential group home. Different instructional sessions in the same day, daily morning and afternoon periods, and several classrooms—workrooms at one site can also serve as settings in a multiple baseline evaluation.

The format of a multiple baseline across persons design is introducing intervention sequentially with two or more individuals. The individuals may present with identical or similar problems within the same or different settings. The design is relevant for independent consultants who routinely receive requests from different referral sources and practitioners employed at an educational and treatment setting who have to respond to an evolving caseload or have training responsibilities with several care-providers.

A strong clinical benefit of multiple baseline designs is being able to detect whether the effects of intervention spread (generalize) to behaviors, settings, and persons that have not been similarly targeted. Measuring generalization lets consultants see if intervention has to be extended or can be delayed or withheld, thereby economizing on time and program planning. From a purely experimental perspective, generalization outcomes are pesky but as noted, clinically desirable and welcome.

Changing Criterion Design. The changing criterion design begins with a baseline phase, followed by intervention that is introduced at some predetermined level and gradually increased or decreased depending on the intervention objective. In the case of a skill acquisition target, an intervention might include positive reinforcement which is presented when a student demonstrates five correct responses, then eight correct responses, then ten correct responses, and so on. The same methodology applies to behavior reduction, for example, an adult displaying problem behaviors which remain at or below a gradually decreasing daily number. The controlling influence of intervention is confirmed when the person's responding closely matches the imposed criteria.

A priority for many consultees is shaping skills and adaptive behaviors of children and adults, hence the attraction of the changing criterion design. Gradually increasing and decreasing select performance measures is also integral to many systems and organizational-change projects. I have found that most consultees readily grasp the logic of the changing criterion design and like the additional feature of not having to repeat (A-B-A-B reversal design) or extend (multiple baseline designs) baseline phases. For these reasons, the changing criterion design may be a consultant's first choice evaluation strategy, at least in cases where the intervention contains a benchmark (criterion) that is gradually changed.

Alternating Treatments Design. Occasionally consultants are called upon to compare the effectiveness of two or more interventions. The alternating treatments design (ATD) is a useful methodology for such evaluation and relatively easy to arrange with some basic planning. The format is to implement different plans, protocols, and procedures in random order and rapid sequence within and/or between successive days. The data paths among the different conditions are compared to evaluate relative effects and select the optimal intervention.

There are many examples of incorporating the ATD in consultation practice. A consultee may have been trying several instructional methods with a child or adult but is unsure about how many of them to use or in what combinations. For example, does the consultee teach most successfully using least-to-most, time-delay, or within-stimulus prompting? Other variations might apply to types of reinforcers, correction procedures, and instructional pacing. Many ATD evaluations can be completed quickly, under natural conditions, and with conclusive findings. The desired outcome from an ATD is choosing one or more interventions a consultee can implement confidently.

Whatever the choice of single-case research design, consultants must convince consultees about the advantages of this evaluation methodology. I always stress that by conducting a controlled evaluation, we can make the best program decisions and reach confident conclusions about intervention effectiveness. With clear explanation, most consultees understand the central logic of single-case designs and how such evaluation contributes to practice. It is also worth emphasizing to consultees that single-case designs are meant to fit with consultation objectives and not the other way around.

SOCIAL VALIDITY

At one time, many years ago, social validity was considered a controversial topic in ABA and a source of considerable debate within the professional community (Kazdin, 1977; Wolf, 1978). Now, assessing social validity is indispensable to program evaluation and expected to be included as a measurement objective in meaningful applied research. Earlier, I described social-validity assessment with consultees to identify the appropriateness of consultation goals at the problem identification phase. In this section, the discussion turns to social-validity assessment of intervention outcomes and the procedures that were used to achieve them.

Social-validity assessment should be conducted with the consumers of consultation services, namely consultees, but also other individuals. For example, although teachers and teacher-assistants may be the direct consumers of school-based consultation, administrators, counselors, and parents of students are indirect consumers of services and can contribute to social-validity assessment. In effect, having the largest pool of consumers and soliciting their attitudes and opinions about intervention procedures and results is the best "quality control" performance feedback a consultant can obtain.

The most objective approach to social-validity assessment is preparing a questionnaire that consultees and other consumers can complete during the intervention evaluation phase. A questionnaire, such as the one displayed in Fig. 7.1, quantifies uniform and divergent assessment findings and collects brief narrative summaries as additional valued information. The following are practical tips for assessing social validity in the context of consultation:

Assess consultee satisfaction with procedures. A questionnaire should include statements that allow consultees to rate their approval of and satisfaction with consultation practices. Ask consultees about the procedures they were trained to implement: Did the procedures produce the desired effects, were the procedures difficult, should the procedures be replicated in similar situations?

Document consultee satisfaction with overall process. Other statements in a questionnaire can address the process of consultation such as the scheduling of site visits, duration of consultee–consultant meetings, consultant availability, and quality of written documents. There is no better way to improve service delivery than asking consultees about these matters.

Keep it brief. A questionnaire should be brief and easy to complete, no more than 8–10 statements, and contained on a single page.

Keep the language simple. Write simple declarative statements such as, "The behavior support plan I implemented with John was effective," or "I learned the skills necessary to conduct discrete trial teaching."

Use a quantitative scale for most questions. Develop a rating scale that can be paired with each statement and reasonably differentiates consultee responses. Most social-validity questionnaires employ a Likert-type scale as follows: 1—strongly disagree, 2—disagree, 3—neither disagree nor agree, 4—agree, 5—strongly agree. A binary scale is also possible (e.g., yes/no, true/false) but will not be as sensitive or informative as having multipoint ratings.

Consider asking for brief written explanations of scores. Some social-validity questionnaires ask consultees to explain the ratings they endorsed for each statement. A brief explanation of, "Why did you

Date:

Setting:

Your name (or anonymous):

Instructions: Please record your opinions about the Behavior Support Plan (BSP) you implemented with Mary during September–November 2017 by checking one rating for each statement. You may add comments about the BSP as well. Thank you!

Statements	Ratings				
	1: Strongly Disagree	2: Disagree	3: Neither Disagree or Agree	4: Agree	5: Strongly Agree
The BSP was easy to understand					
If you selected Ratings #1 or #2, please explain:					
The BSP procedures were easy to implement					
If you selected Ratings #1 or #2, please explain:					
The BSP properly addressed intervention objectives					
If you selected Ratings #1 or #2, please explain:					
The student responded positively to the BSP					
If you selected Ratings #1 or #2, please explain:					
I was trained effectively to implement the BSP					
If you selected Ratings #1 or #2, please explain:					
I would recommend the BSP for other students					
If you selected Ratings #1 or #2, please explain					
Additional comments, if any:					

Figure 7.1 Social-validity assessment questionnaire.

select this rating," can be clarifying and is not effortful as long as the statements stay at a 8–10 limit.

Ask for narrative feedback. Leave space on the social-validity questionnaire for consultees to write in any comments or additional feedback. This can be accomplished with a summary section at the bottom of the page that requests "Additional thoughts and suggestions, if any."

Give the option of anonymity. Allow consultees the option of recording their name on the questionnaire or completing it anonymously.

Be specific about time. Specify the time period that is being assessed, for example, "The six months during which you implemented Kathy's specialized instructional program" or "The months you received consultation services at home."

Explain the social validity process. Organize procedures to explain, distribute, and collect completed social-validity questionnaires. The most straightforward explanation is that as a consultant, you are interested in what the recipients of your services think about the work that was accomplished. Discuss further that the questionnaire is not an evaluation of their performance and that their ratings have nothing to do with job appraisal. Be clear that their opinions are solely intended to make you a better consultant.

Decide how surveys are delivered and collected. After explaining the social-validity questionnaire to consultees in a group meeting, you can distribute it to them, request that they respond independently, and immediately thereafter return the completed version to you. The advantages of this approach is that it ensures consultees do not collaborate about their opinions and you are guaranteed a 100% return rate. The downside is that consultees may be inclined to only endorse positive ratings, that is, produce biased responses due to reactivity occasioned by the presence of the consultant.

Alternatively, the consultant can distribute the social-validity questionnaire and ask that consultees return it completed by a specified deadline. The consultant can arrange to pick up the completed questionnaires individually from consultees at a deadline date or they can deposit them in a designated location. This approach does not control for possible conferencing among consultees and some questionnaires may not be returned on time. Distributing and returning the questionnaire via email is another option but may not be pleasing to consultees who wish to respond anonymously. Alternatively, free web-based survey services can be used and can facilitate anonymity.

Analyze your social-validity data. Upon summarizing the completed social-validity questionnaires, a consultant should categorize ratings that were consistently high, low, or equivocal along the dimensions of satisfaction, acceptability, and effectiveness. In an ideal world, it would be helpful to then meet with consultees and have them elaborate on their feedback, gaining further insight into consultation services that were rated less favorably and seeking suggestions for improvement. However, many consultees will not be comfortable in a postassessment meeting that emphasizes in-person performance feedback directed at a consultant! Therefore, the endorsed questionnaire ratings and any written comments from consultees may have to suffice for obtaining feedback and informing practice directions.

MAINTENANCE

Measuring the long-term effects of behavioral consultation is yet another facet of intervention evaluation. Consultees and the people who requested consultation services want to know if their efforts with children and adults produce outcomes that are lasting and can be maintained. Consultants also want to know how consultees perform after services with them terminate.

For many consultants, opportunities to evaluate response maintenance are hindered because the time allotted to a case referral or systems project is limited. Time constraints may be the result of the conditions set forth in a services contract, restrictions on caseload, or competing service demands. Other situations may allow a consultant to stay involved for a longer period of time and be able to conduct maintenance evaluation. I recommend you explicitly state in your initial negotations regarding the consultation relationship, process, and fees, that maintenance and follow-up be included in your services, if at all possible.

Definitions of response maintenance vary across different publications and from consultant to consultant. The performance of individuals "post-intervention" is one definition. However, does post-intervention mean without any intervention, with variation of a previous intervention, or intervention that has been faded but not removed completely? Most consultants are familiar with cases and projects in which intervention must be continued at full strength indefinitely and there is never a true post-intervention phase. Other times, post-intervention is associated with intervention implementation that is not as intensive as applied initially but still in effect. I have found that elimination of previously effective intervention while maintaining long-term success is rare.

Several years ago, I wrote: "The issue of maintenance should be considered from the earliest stages of treatment formulation and implementation....an active process of maintenance facilitation that entails the adjustment of treatment procedures so that an individual's skill performance and behavior are sustained under conditions that approximate 'real world' contingencies" (Luiselli, 1998, p. 74). My message, then and now, is that as soon as positive effects from procedures, plans, and recommendations are realized, consultants should consider how intervention will be dismantled. That is, we should look at intervention and maintenance contemporaneously, each requiring systematic planning, application, and evaluation.

In working with consultees to advise them on their instructional and behavior-support interventions with children and adults, the following strategies are appropriate for promoting response maintenance:

- Gradually "thin" reinforcement from continuous to intermittent schedules.
- Shift reinforcement from tangible stimuli to social consequences, while remaining relevant to behavioral function.
- Delay presentation of reinforcement.
- Slowly decrease the intensity of care-provider supervision.
- If warranted, teach self-management and self-control.
- Systematically withdraw procedures comprising a multicomponent intervention plan.

When consultation is directed at systems-level projects, the steps towards maintenance programming are to assess what resources are needed at an educational and treatment setting and how they can be provided to sustain performance. For example, I have been involved in several consultation projects at human services organizations that had the goal of improving the frequency, quality, and effects of supervision by senior clinicians and behavior analysts. We designed, implemented, and evaluated several performance-improvement projects that had positive findings. One of the approaches to facilitating maintenance of the projects was choosing procedures which the supervisors could implement faithfully and they approved as being acceptable. Other planned maintenance supports were adjusting supervisor responsibilities in response to changes in their caseloads, scheduling organizational project-review meetings, and preparing a handbook that standardized procedures for current and future supervisors. In several of these projects, maintenance evaluations revealed that these supports were effective and durable.

CHAPTER SUMMARY

- Single-case designs are integral to clinical practice and intervention evaluation.
- Select and adapt single-case designs to consultation objectives, target behaviors, and setting characteristics.
- Design social-validity questionnaires to assess consultee and indirect consumer opinions about intervention satisfaction and acceptability.
- Introduced maintenance-promotion strategies during intervention.
- Make maintenance evaluation a major activity of consultation service delivery.

CHAPTER 8

Supervision

The best consultants I have known and worked with were also skilled supervisors. Being hired as a consultant necessarily requires supervision of consultees throughout consultation phases, as reviewed in earlier chapters. The role of a supervisor is also paramount for full-time practitioners who consult to staff at educational and treatment settings. Many consultants (myself included) were not trained to become a competent supervisor but acquired skills on-the-job, through continuing education, and, if lucky, by having influential role models along the way. Thankfully, that situation has changed for the better with increased attention to supervisor standards and practices taught in graduate school, internship, and postdoctoral training programs.

Another venue for consultants is supervising individuals working toward professional certifications such as a licensed psychologist and behavior analyst. For example, the BACB requires that aspiring BCBAs and BCaBAs receive designated hours of weekly supervision that are proportionately adjusted to fieldwork hours and experience standards (BACB, 2017). Supervisors must be BACB approved and complete (1) an 8-h supervision training course, (2) experience standards training module, and (3) annual continuing education training workshops. The increasing need for and credentialing of behavior analysts means that professionals meeting these training requirements should be able to devote a portion of their consultation services to supervision.

Several suggested guidelines for conducting BACB supervision have been published, including general competencies (Turner, 2017; Turner, Fischer, & Luiselli, 2016), supervising individually and in groups (Sellers, Valentino, & LeBlanc, 2016; Valentino, Sellers, & LeBlanc, 2016), and dealing with ethical dilemmas that arise during supervision (Sellers, Alai-Rosales, & MacDonald, 2016). I note that these guidelines are not exclusive to behavior analytic supervision but apply equally as well to nonbehavioral practitioners and consultees. What

Conducting Behavioral Consultation in Educational and Treatment Settings.
DOI: https://doi.org/10.1016/B978-0-12-814445-9.00008-0

has emerged and continues to evolve are empirically informed methods for training consultants to implement supervision effectively in the best interests of supervisor and supervisee alike.

GETTING STARTED

Providing quality supervision is time-consuming and extends well beyond face-to-face encounters. Time must be allotted to observations, preparing written materials (e.g., suggested readings), correspondence, evaluating permanent products, and communicating with other individuals who have responsibilities with the consultee. There is also the time spent commuting to and from the settings where supervision takes place. Seen in this light, a consultant who agrees to supervise one consultee for 1 h each week in actuality will be looking at more than the required 4 h of supervision per month, likely twice that amount of time and maybe more. When additional consultees must be supervised, these time demands only increase.

Before establishing supervisory relationships, be sure your schedule allows for the necessary time and then some. Anticipate more work than what appears to be on the surface. Carefully review the schedule of supervision sessions and be exact about the locations of supervision. These planning strategies may be less of an issue for in-house practitioners than independent consultants but are pertinent nonetheless. Keep in mind that common reasons for consultee and supervisee dissatisfaction is supervisors who do not keep to a prearranged schedule, arrive late to supervision sessions, cheat on time, and are disorganized.

GOALS AND EXPECTATIONS

Like other consultation activities, it is imperative that a consultant and consultee establish mutual supervision goals and expectations. Discussions should start as soon as formal supervision begins by each person voicing her/his priorities and achieving consensus. From the perspective of the consultee, high-ranking goals and expectations will often concern learning particular skills such as implementing instructional methods, conducting assessments, writing intervention plans, recording data, and evaluating program effectiveness. Many consultees are also interested in on-the-job goals and expectations that their employer desires, some of which can be addressed through supervision.

For consultees who are seeking licensure and certification, the goals and expectations of supervision will be closely tied to the requirements of the respective credentialing organization. Most relevant to readers of this guidebook are consultees being supervised towards state licensure in psychology, certification as a school psychologist (NASP), and board certification in behavior analysis (BACB). Consultants should be fully versed in and capable of following these supervision guidelines. The guidelines define the percentage of consultee service delivery that must be supervised, content of supervision, individual and group supervision formats, documentation, and many other requirements.

Some credentialing organizations such as the BACB require an approved and signed contract between supervisor and supervisee. A contract sets the conditions for supervision and describes the professional relationship in terms of responsibilities and performance. Not all supervision arrangements between a consultant and consultee demand a contract but it is a good idea to spell out the goals and expectations in writing and with formality. Be prepared for some of these goals and expectations to change as supervision continues.

INTERACTIONS WITH CONSULTEES

Many consultees may have never participated in formal supervision. So, in addition to assessing their training needs and agreeing about the purposes of supervision, consultants should ask the following question: "What can I do to make supervision as comfortable as possible?" This question has multiple layers but is grounded in several operating principles.

Always consider the consultees best interests. As the consultant-supervisor, your role is to do what is best for the consultee. Yes, you have more expertise, cannot overlook training needs, must follow best practice guidelines, and in most cases, will be viewed as an authority. And yet, good supervision, indeed the best supervision, is not defined by what you think of the person you are supervising but instead, what that person thinks about you.

Set consultee goals. Work persistently with consultees to select and refine their performance goals by writing an achievable training plan, monitoring progress, and reinforcing achievement. So much of supervision is *shaping* gradual behavior change towards personalized objectives that are most meaningful to the consultee.

Model the behavior you want to see. Demonstrate the behavior you want from consultees: a positive attitude, conversational, nondictatorial, reflective, sensitive to individual differences, confident, uniformly pleasant. Lest you think that this is an unrealistic and nonattainable list, recall your own supervisors and their qualities you most admired—the same should apply to your supervisory profile.

Consider style of supervision. Some consultees need and want firm direction from a supervisor, telling them what to do and what not to do with few options. Other consultees prefer a degree of autonomy when responding to supervisor recommendations. And, as I have seen, there are consultees who will set their own agenda, prepared with care, and look for the supervisor to approve. An effective supervisor must evaluate the motivations and existing skills of each consultee before initiating a training plan that is strategic and will yield favorable results.

Be observant and open. First impressions can be deceiving. The initially quiet and reserved consultee may gradually become more vocal and confident. Other consultees appear strident and self-assured when in reality their skills are not so formative. Consultants must be perceptive enough to detect interpersonal strengths and weaknesses among consultees and mentor accordingly during supervision.

Demonstrate respect for consultee's personal life circumstances. Learn about a consultee's life outside of the practice setting, gradually, through self-disclosure, and only to offer support and guidance. For example, consultees may have childcare responsibilities, be taking classes, work a second job, or commute long distances. These and many other life circumstances are just as meaningful as the competency training goals addressed in supervision. A supervisor who is sensitive to "lifestyle management" resonates well.

Be upbeat. To reiterate and expand upon a previous point, have a pleasant and welcoming demeanor, with stable mood, energy, and deportment every time you meet for supervision with a consultee. If a supervisor's presentation changes from session to session, it will affect how consultees respond to and value what you have to offer.

The supervisor is a role model and must demonstrate consistent actions and attitudes that consultees can appreciate and emulate in day-to-day performance. It is important to keep in mind the distinction between private events and overt behavior, that is, one does not directly cause the other. If we feel anxious or frustrated, it may be tempting to believe that we *are* anxious or frustrated and therefore that it may not be possible to appear civil and constructive. It can be effective to actively practice reminding oneself that, if you value being an effective supervisor and leader, then behave constructively at all times.

ETHICS

Consultants should be prepared to confront many ethical challenges in their supervision of consultees (Bailey & Burch, 2016). It is a mistake to assume that questions about ethics are rare occasions and unlikely to be encountered during consultation. In reality, ethical dilemmas occur all the time, will appear in supervision, and cannot be overlooked. I see four areas that dominate the ethics landscape

Consultee ethical knowledge. Consultants are well-advised to give considerable thought to how their consultees approach, understand, and resolve ethical dilemmas. Toward this end, consultees require knowledge about prevailing ethics codes and guidance that is informed by previous experience guiding decision-making. A useful practice is for the consultant to present hypothetical ethical dilemmas to consultees throughout supervision and focus on applicable problem-solving strategies. Posing examples and fictional illustrations is valuable because many consultees may not be aware of conditions and events that rise to the level of ethical concern. Other consultees may be uncertain about possible ethical violations and need clarification through representative (teaching) examples.

Ethics strategies for supervisors. Consultants must be aware of their ethical behavior when delivering supervision. All professional ethics codes identify actions that are patently unethical: inappropriate relationships with clients, fraudulent activities, violation of confidentiality, improper sharing-distribution of personal health information, and practicing without a license-certification. The following are some additional and useful risk management precautions:

Scope of competence. Only supervise in areas defined by your practice competencies. Competency applies to diagnostic populations, assessment methodologies, intervention methods, types of evaluation, and cultural groups commensurate with a consultant's training and experience. Becoming competent in particular areas of supervision can be approached through continuing education, specialty training, mentoring, and related avenues of professional development. Consultants should decline supervision referrals and requests whenever there are doubts about competency demands and expectations.

Supervisor culpability. A supervisor will be held responsible for the actions of supervisees. This caveat means that a consultant must be certain that consultees have the skills necessary to perform implementation recommendations proficiently. Effective risk management in this regard begins by spelling out a consultee's performance criteria and requirements. This skills assessment will determine whether additional training is needed in order for a consultee to practice properly and ensure that the supervising consultant has behaved ethically.

Supervisor caseload. Pragmatic considerations should not be neglected when conducting supervision, for example, only taking on as many consultees as time permits, adhering to the supervisory requirements of credentialing agencies, and resisting coercive directives or financial incentives to supervise an unrealistic number of consultees. Overburdened supervisors are ineffective supervisors and prone to otherwise preventable ethical mishaps.

Goals and progress monitoring. Conscientiously monitor the effects of your supervision with consultees. This activity begins by keeping observation and session notes which document progress towards the goals and expectations that were mutually established at the onset of supervision. Delivering performance feedback to consultees is another element of progress monitoring and an indispensable risk management strategy. Supervisor feedback through reinforcement and correction aims to build the skills a consultee needs for practicing competently. When skills improve and service outcomes are achieved, the consultant responsible for supervision has achieved a high ethical standard.

Trainee: Placement Site
Supervisor: Evaluation Period:

Supervision Arrangement		
Measures	YES	NO or NOT ALWAYS: Explain
Supervision sessions occur as scheduled		
Supervision sessions start and end on time		
Supervision sessions are free of distractions		
Supervision sessions can be re-scheduled as warranted		
I am able to correspond with my supervisor between supervision sessions		

Supervisor Behavior					
Measures	Rarely		Sometimes		Always
	1	2	3	4	5
Supervisor is approachable					
Supervisor is attentive to my current abilities and training needs					
Supervisor gives me behavior-specific positive feedback about my strengths					
Supervisor gives me behavior-specific corrective feedback about my weaknesses					
Supervisor gives clear performance expectations and evaluation procedures					
Supervisor models professional behavior (clinical decision making, ethics, confidentiality)					
Supervisor models technical skills					
Supervisor requires me to practice (e.g., role play) when learning new skills					
Supervisor delivers feedback in a variety of modalities (e.g., verbal, written, graphic)					
Supervisor reviews my written work					
Supervisor facilitates my critical thinking					
Supervisor shows support and positive regard					
Supervisor listens well					
Supervisor shows energy and enthusiasm					

Figure 8.1 Supervision Monitoring and Evaluation Form.

Social validity. Further documentation of supervision effectiveness comes from social validity assessment of consultees. In Turner et al. (2016), were referenced a *Supervision Monitoring and Evaluation Form*, shown in Fig. 8.1. The form was developed to measure satisfaction ratings of fifth-year graduate students enrolled in a doctoral internship program in clinical psychology. Interns completed the form twice per year, met with

Supervisor is able to shift focus during sessions as warranted					
Supervisor is prepared for supervision sessions					
Supervisor advises about my professional development					
Supervisor suggests and/or assigns up to date readings and other materials					

Supervision Content					
Measures	Rarely		Sometimes		Always
	1	2	3	4	5
Supervision addresses the BACB Task List and ethical and professional guidelines of the field					
Supervision is a collaborative experience					
Supervision informs me about evidence-based practices					
Supervision addresses objectives in my individualized training plan					
Supervision builds and enhances my clinical skills (e.g., case conceptualization)					
Supervision expands my knowledge base					
Supervision considers matters of diversity and inclusion					
Supervision is conducted within the boundaries of confidentiality					
Supervision advises helpfully about my clinical interactions with clients, constituents and other service providers					
Supervision fortifies my professional development					
Supervision enhances my ability to make clinical decisions and solve problems					

Please complete this form and review it with your supervisor during your next scheduled session. Use the space below to note any additional comments or discussion points.

Trainee Signature:		Date:
Supervisor Signature:		Date:

Figure 8.1 Continued

their supervisors to review the ratings, and decided on action plans to correct any acknowledged deficiencies within the categories of supervision arrangement, supervisor behavior, and supervision content. Both consultants and consultees can contribute to designing such a form as a collaborative effort that guards against the risks of failing to provide effective and ethically responsible supervision.

Ethical dilemmas. The third area of ethical concentration is how consultants should react to uncomfortable situations that appear during supervision. The following scenarios illustrate two possible ethical dilemmas:

> Dr. Smith is a licensed psychologist who consults to several public schools in the same district. His consultation activities include supervising three classroom teachers implementing behavior support plans with difficult students. He is concerned that one of the teachers lacks instructional skills, sometimes makes derogatory comments in class, resists consultation recommendations, and misapplies behavioral intervention procedures. He has addressed these issues with the teacher during supervision and spoke confidentially with the school principal, who told him, "That's just the way she is, try to work around it." Dr. Smith was dissatisfied with the principal's response and believes he is ethically obliged to contact the Superintendent of Schools.

> Julie is a supervising behavior analyst at a residential program for children with developmental disabilities. The program publicizes its orientation as multidisciplinary and committed to "an ABA methodology and philosophy." However, after several months at the program Julie realizes that many of the consultees she supervises are not skilled behavioral practitioners and the program as a whole does not provide services as advertised. She witnesses consultees implementing nonevidence supported procedures, poorly designed interventions, and methods that deviate from conventional ABA practices. Julie has expressed her impressions with consultees in supervision and concluded that they have not received adequate and proper ABA training, nor does the program have the necessary clinical expertise. Under these circumstances, she does not think that her supervision can be effective and has grave concerns about how the program operates and is portrayed.

The preceding illustrations reveal a common challenge that consultants face when conducting supervision. Displayed in Fig. 8.2, events begin when a consultant observes or gains knowledge about the actions and questionable professional behavior of consultees and associated care-providers. Often, the question that arises has to do with perceived incompetence that approaches or qualifies as unacceptable practice according to the consultant's prevailing ethics codes. Steps must be taken if and when she/he judges that an ethical violation has occurred.

Determining an ethical violation is complicated because professional ethics codes provide limited guidance about resolving

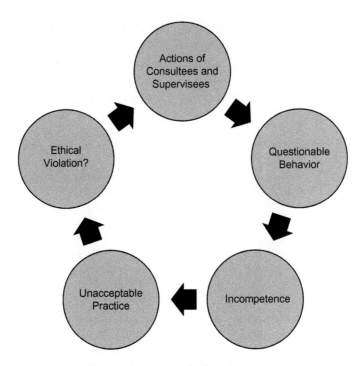

Figure 8.2 Common sequence of identifying possible ethical violations.

dilemmas. Questions about ethical violations are rarely simple and transparent or can be answered dogmatically. It is more often the case that individual judgement is necessary in applying ethics codes to professional practice. There is also an ethical-moral versus legal distinction wherein codes of ethics may require a more stringent standard of conduct than the law prescribes. Finally, consultants delivering supervision may never have been confronted with an ethical challenge, received limited training in the area, and face the burden of "going it alone."

Taking action on ethical matters. The fourth area of ethics in supervision is deciding what to do once a suspected violation seems apparent. Below is a problem-solving checklist gleaned from several professional ethics codes and presented in sequential first-to-last order:

Carefully identify the presenting ethical dilemma. Does the issue at hand fall within your ethics code and standards of competent practice? Take sufficient time to deliberate on this matter before deciding on further action.

Review the ethics principles that apply. The principles may be expressed in direct actions you have observed or been informed about. Always seek to corroborate your impressions from multiple sources who are in a position to respond reliably.

Confer with trusted colleagues. Seek the opinions of colleagues and your own supervisors outside of the consultation setting. Much can be gained by tapping into an independent and objective perspective.

Evaluate the prevailing conditions. Be sure to thoroughly evaluation the conditions that may have contributed to a potential ethical violation. You want to dispassionately assess the rights-welfare of the affected parties before forming an action plan.

Set forth multiple solutions. Think about as many possible solutions that could resolve the problem. Use a "brainstorming" approach by writing down all reasonable resolution options.

Perform a risk–benefit analysis. Supplement your proposed solutions by describing the best and worst possible outcomes.

Present your concerns. Speak to the consultees you are supervising, explaining your perspective, asking for their interpretation, and working towards a correction plan.

Last options. In cases where collegial problem-solving with a consultee is unsuccessful, plan to *implement more robust tactics* such as bringing your concerns to administrators or filing a formal complaint with a credentialing agency.

CHAPTER SUMMARY

- Most consultants will have a supervisory role with consultees.
- Carefully review time demands and other practical considerations involved with supervision.
- Establish mutual supervision goals and expectations with consultees.
- Prepare a written training plan that can be reviewed, monitored, and revised with consultees during supervision.
- Study the interpersonal and learning style of consultees to make supervision appealing and productive.
- Model caring, responsive, receptive, and thoughtful behavior consistently with consultees.
- Be fully informed about ethics codes pertaining to supervision, risk management strategies, and problem-solving approaches for dealing with and resolving ethical dilemmas.

CHAPTER 9

Likeability, Performance Management, and Conflict Resolution

The content of previous chapters emphasized consultation practices and competencies within consultation phases. I reviewed effective implementation guidelines, evaluation methods, and steps for conducting observations, supervision, and assessment of intervention integrity and social validity. This chapter reintroduces in broader context some key determinants to consultation success, specifically consultant likeability and performance management. Another section of the chapter looks at common conflict situations which can arise during consultation and recommended approaches to conflict resolution.

LIKEABILITY

Consultees should like the consultants they work with. From a strictly learning theory perspective, consultants want to function as conditioned reinforcers whom consultees readily approach, value, trust, and respect. In this guidebook, likeability was considered in the chapters that described strategies for building consultant–consultee relationships, conducting meetings, delivering performance feedback, and supervising. The influence of likeability is so pertinent to consultation practice that more detailed analysis is warranted.

When leading consultation training workshops and seminars, I always include a segment that poses the question, "What factors contribute to a consultant's likeability?" Virtually every attendee agrees that likeability is a valid concept, can be defined operationally, and predicts consultation success. They also consistently generate a list of likeability characteristics that competent consultants display.

Demeanor. Having a calm and relaxed demeanor has an immediate effect upon everyone in the room. The consultant smiles, sits and stands without rigid body posture, speaks in a pleasant tone, and is

Conducting Behavioral Consultation in Educational and Treatment Settings.
DOI: https://doi.org/10.1016/B978-0-12-814445-9.00009-2

conscious of such behavior at all times. Consultants who do not behave this way or do so inconsistently will not gain favor among consultees or be seen in a positive light. Present yourself in a manner that encourages approach and not avoidance.

Dress appropriately. Appearance counts, however much some people discount this likeability characteristic. What will consultees and other people in the education and treatment setting think about the quality of your work if you appear disheveled, unkempt, and poorly groomed? Do you feel comfortable with a personal physician, attorney, financial advisor, or similar professional who looks like she/he is about to mow the lawn or workout at the gym? You should convey respect for the individuals receiving your services by always dressing and preparing yourself professionally. Your clothing does not have to be expensive and should not be ostentatious but clean, coordinated, and fitting the surroundings. A business casual look will be appropriate for many settings, while a "dress up mode" would be the choice for more formal activities such as school—family conferences and multidisciplinary meetings. Thoughtful grooming is also a prerequisite lest you appear as the well-dressed consultant with hair askew, dirty fingernails, and bad breath. As a supervisor of mine once said, make it a point to spend some time with your appearance in mind.

Listen attentively. We can usually tell when persons we are speaking to are not paying attention and appear disinterested in conversation. They look away, ignore comments, fidget, are easily distracted, and excessively dictate the discussion. Another characteristic of a poor listener is interrupting such that you the speaker, cannot complete a sentence. These behaviors are precisely what consultants should not do when talking with consultees. Keep the focus of conversational exchanges on the consultee by maintaining eye-contact, staying on topic, and resisting the temptation to control the dialogue. One of the best qualities of attentive listeners I have observed is that they *do not talk* while other persons are speaking: just wait quietly, allow the speaker to finish, pause a few seconds, and resume conversation. This wait-to-speak and noninterruptive awareness has a demonstrable effect on being recognized as a good listener.

Nonjudgmental. A consultant has to be a keen observer, tactician, and evaluator, forming opinions about people and settings, and making informed decisions. Yes, judgment is involved when conducting a risk—benefit analysis, choosing one of several possible interventions, and many other consultant decisions. Being judgmental is something different; a negative, critical, poorly developed, and often presumptuous opinion about someone's beliefs and behavior. Being judgmental puts consultees in a bad light and taints interactions negatively. This effect is untenable because consultants have to work with consultees who are hired employees at an educational and treatment setting. The consultant does not pick, retain, or dismiss these individuals. Behaving nonjudgmentally means accepting each consultee at her/his skill level and implementing consultation practices that are instructive, supportive, socially valid, and not constrained by misinformed attitudes.

Emotional stability. I once had a supervisor whose affect changed week to week, session to session, sometimes within the same session or during a lengthy interaction. He was variably happy and sad, calm and angry, responsive and confrontative, engaged and withdrawn. I spent a great deal of time trying to adapt to his erratic behavior but even more time attempting to understand why he acted this way. I was never successful.

My experience with this supervisor and a few similar individuals during my career taught me the importance of demonstrating emotional stability as a consultant. The mood and affect of a consultant is what consultees notice first. Instability and uncertainty about what a consultant thinks and feels makes consultees uncomfortable, questioning themselves, and assuming they are to blame for the perceived discord. Consultees cannot learn and improve performance if the people advising them do not demonstrate emotional stability. Do not let events outside the educational and treatment setting or personal challenges influence interactions with consultees. Be mindful of maintaining a consistent and predictable decorum whenever engaged in consultation practices. This mandate does not mean overlooking or disregarding one's emotional health and well-being, rather taking steps to guard against intrusion from personal life challenges.

For example, take time to assess sources of stress and conflict that may impinge on your work with consultees. Set performance goals and solutions to overcome these unwanted influences. Such strategies include referring to checklist reminders of "best behaviors" to display in the company of consultees. Get in the habit of practicing highly valued interpersonal skills when away from the consultation setting. If warranted, adjust your consultation activities when your mind and body are so taxed that the ill effects could compromise interactions with consultees. Adopt a prevention focus achieved through self-assessment and demonstrated convincingly on the job.

Know the subject matter. However valuable interpersonal and communication skills are in being liked and accepted by consultees, a consultant must be able to impart knowledge and expertise in order to be valued. I do not imply showing off intellectually by reciting the research literature, speaking in highly technical language, or performing other gestures that are intended to impress listeners. Most consultees will turn off to pedantic demonstrations and can quickly discern a consultant's true expertise. An accurate perception of knowledge results when consultants are unequivocally devoted to the welfare of consultees and their activities within educational and treatment settings. It shows that you know the subject matter when you follow a few simple guidelines:

- Answer questions clearly without pontificating.
- Support recommendations using empirical case examples.
- Focus on practice and not theory.
- Acknowledge what you do not know.
- Deliver a consistent message.
- Listen respectfully to alternative opinions.
- Do not stray from boundaries of competence.

Be dependable. Being dependable equates to following through with committed actions, in other words, displaying "say-do" correspondence. Dependable consultants arrive on time to appointments, keep their scheduled obligations, produce written documents as promised, return telephone calls and emails, and make themselves available at off-hours. This likeability factor is always at the top of the list of highly rated consultant attributes. Dependable performance begins by setting consultation practice priorities with individuals, groups, and systems-levels projects. The process of building consensus among consultees at every consultation phase establishes one or more objectives that a consultant can rank order by priority and, in turn, determine where dependability is most prominent. In illustration, consultation services may be directed at an emergency risk assessment, time-limited intervention planning at a school, implementation of a care-provider training program, or project development towards organizational clinical safety. Consultants must be able to complete performance tasks dependably as dictated by the identified priorities and respective time deadlines.

Humor. Pleasant interactions with consultees invariably involve laughter and humor. A humorless consultant does not smile and seems to take life too seriously, which is off-putting to most people. Of course, the work in educational and treatment settings is serious and should not be taken lightly. However, a difficult day and the intense focus of consultation services are easier to handle with a laugh and lighthearted perspective. What is not simple but perplexingly complex is defining universally humorous topics, using humor appropriately, and recognizing when humor is ill advised.

Sometimes humor will be appropriately encountered during mundane experiences such as an adult recalling a funny scene from a movie or a child showing off a clever Halloween costume. Consultees may laugh about their bland activities over the weekend. Or, the source of laughter may be conversations concerning a surprise birthday party, events on a family vacation, or noncontroversial news events. In these social conditions it would be odd not to laugh in the company of consultees and risk being perceived as a stogy and uptight professional. But, the greater risk is making remarks and jokes which, intended to be humorous, are offensive to the recipients of consultation services.

My strong advice is to put humor on the backburner. Do not try to be a comedian, do not talk about any subject that is remotely risqué, and do not join forces with individuals who demonstrate questionable taste. A good general rule is to not make jokes about maladaptive behaviors, diagnoses, or any persons involved in consultation. In short, smile and be happy about the work being done, enhancing relationships with consultees, but always approaching humor with sensitivity and caution.

PERFORMANCE MANAGEMENT

Most performance specialists write and speak about time management as the key to improving productivity. My interpretation is that we do not actually manage time but more our performance during the time accessible to us. Time advances regardless of what we do. We do not control time, stopping and starting at our discretion. And we do not save time in some depository for later use.

Effective performance management by consultants is no different from applying successful strategies with consultees. The many activities performed by consultants during the five-phase problem-solving model have to be implemented competently, with integrity, and leading to desirable outcomes for consultees and service-recipients. There are several performance management strategies every consultant should strive to master.

Scheduling. I would be unable to function professionally without my appointment book. My preference is the hand-written, "week-at-a-glance" format that I can open and display on my desk and carry with me when away from the office. Some people, maybe you, are partial towards electronic scheduling and planning systems available on personal computers, smartphones, and platform devices. Whatever the medium, the performance objective is to faithfully record a daily, weekly, and monthly schedule. The following is a list of tips to consider for scheduling:

- Scheduling should include reoccurring meetings, supervision sessions, observations, and related activities that typically occur at the same time and on the same day (e.g., Tuesday: Clinical Team Meeting (10:00–11:00 a.m.)). Fixed schedule commitments are predictable and form the structure for fitting-in new consultation referrals and assignments.
- Be aware of the time preparing for, transitioning to, and initiating consultation activities when constructing a schedule. Factoring commute time between educational and treatment settings is particularly relevant for independent consultants who must travel to multiple locations but just as important for practitioners who visit several program sites within a human services-behavioral healthcare organization.
- Periodically conduct a time-study to evaluate distribution of activities that comprise your consultation schedule. Performance can be improved by making some often overlooked schedule changes. For example, two, half-day consultation visits each week in the same public school district might be better scheduled on one day. A detailed schedule review may reveal that the duration of some meetings with consultees can be reduced without sacrificing

effectiveness. Performance will improve by discovering these time savings.

- Integrate planning time into your schedule, that is, time you spend by yourself in an office, home, library, or community location to manage operational details of consultation practice. These scheduled periods may be set aside to respond to nonurgent email correspondence and telephone calls, prepare and review to do lists (see below), read publications, or simply serve as an outlet for personal reflection. Too often, consultants try to manage these activities on the run and in the midst of crowded days that only limit performance. Scheduled planning time alone is almost always neglected despite the positive effect it has on performance management.

- Plan next day activities the night before, followed by another schedule review in the morning. Through advance scheduled planning, a consultant avoids harried decision-making, knows the day's activities ahead of time, and can have ready any materials that may be necessary.

To do lists. To do lists are an indispensable guide to performance management. For optimal effectiveness, a to do list should have action items within three categories. *Immediate* action items reflect tasks and activities to be completed that day. *Intermediate* action items are tasks and activities that have to be completed by a later deadline during the week. *Long-term* action items are tasks and activities within a lengthier timeframe, usually time-sensitive project proposals, formal presentations, submission of evaluation reports, and so on.

The advantages of to do lists start with the performance-enhancing effect of writing down goals and not relying on memory or less objective planning guides. Assigning action plans to immediate, intermediate, and long-term categories imposes deadlines that help allocate time needed for completion. The list of completed action items is also a measure of performance effectiveness. Something I would add is the reinforcement contacted when checking "done" action items on a to do list!

The action items you record on a to do list must be manageable. Some useful tips for using to do lists for task management include:

- Accurately define the priority level of action items.
- Set completion deadlines.

- Document completion criteria (what exactly has to be accomplished?).
- Determine whether additional resources are needed to achieve performance expectations.

Further, preparation of a to do list is not a one-time event. You manage action items by reviewing your to do list several times daily, adding, removing, and transferring items according to their planning, ongoing, and completion status. In this way, the to do list becomes a fluid document on pace with a consultant's ever-shifting priorities.

In the office. Office time for consultants is precious and should be scheduled as fastidiously as time spent in the field. I have always found it valuable to schedule office hours for select time periods and on specific days in the week. Activities in the office are many and can only be accomplished by eliminating distractions and other time-wasters. Tips for making the most of office time include:

- Unless a portion of time in the office entails electronic correspondence and Internet access purely devoted to consultation practice, eliminate social media as a source of distraction. Do not intrude on productivity by compulsively checking your accounts and communication threads. Turn off devices that are not needed to complete your work.
- Resist answering your phone when it rings during office hours and allow calls to go to voicemail. Alerting consultees and other callers that you will not be answering your phone during designated times of the day will also promote productivity in the office.
- If your consultation activities within private practice or an organization include administrative support, tell staff to inform unscheduled office visitors that you cannot be interrupted. The venerable "do not disturb" sign posted on your office door is another remedy as long as you tactfully explain its appearance and stay true to the message.

Paperwork. Much of the paperwork, writing, reading, and clerical tasks that consume consultants take place in the office. There are hardcopy and electronic documents to complete, edit, distribute, and file. Completed data recording forms must be summarized, aggregated, and archived. Poor and haphazard organization of these materials is a major distraction and deters productivity when you have to perform tasks such as locate a particular document or source information, pull up a report for immediate attention, send a behavior support plan, submit a service invoice, construct a graph from raw data forms, and the like.

To better manage efficiency, organize hardcopy and electronic files-folders by distinct labels which correspond to your dominant consultation activities. These designations might include but are not limited to (1) Evaluation Reports, (2) Instructional Protocols, (3) Behavior Support Plans, (4) Data Recording Forms, (5) Supervision Notes, (6) Meeting Summaries, (7) Correspondence, and (8) Systems Projects. If consultation is with consultees and a single child or adult, multiple documents can be contained in one folder with her/his name. Other multidocument files-folders can be prepared according to superordinate headings with the name of the educational and treatment setting, project title, or litigation case number. Whatever the system, the goal is to have "one-stop shopping" anytime you need to retrieve documents and records.

Another organizational aid is creating a list, prominently displayed on either a bulletin board or computer desktop, naming the location of each file-folder. For example, hardcopy data summaries for "Berkshire Training Program" are contained in "File Drawer #2" behind the tab labeled "Projects." Electronic documents pertinent to school consultation are found in the computer desktop folder "2017−2018," containing the subfolder "Consultation Contracts," making available a second subfolder titled "Hampstead School District." This type of graphic organizer saves countless hours searching for information that can be gathered far more efficiently.

CONFLICT RESOLUTION

The problem-solving foundation of behavioral consultation is constructed with conflict resolution in mind. Conflicts can and do arise between and among consultees, administrators, supervisors, and consultants. Although conflicts should be expected throughout the five-phase consultation model, a consultant's role in resolution will vary depending on the sources of conflict, the impact of conflict on service delivery, viable decision-making, and follow through.

The sources of conflict during consultation are many. Consultees may disagree with a consultant's understanding of the referral problem (s). With consultees working on a project team, they might question the reason for consultation input. It is often the case that consultees disagree and reject consultant recommendations and suggested practices. Consultants can and must confront such scenarios head-on, ideally through the preventive and problem-solving strategies presented in earlier chapters of this guidebook, noting the steps below:

Be decisive. Conflict resolution begins when a consultant identifies the origins of disagreement and disapproval. Avoiding or ignoring conflict does not lead to resolution.

Time urgency. Evaluate the intensity of apparent conflict. Does it demand immediate attention or can you pause for a period of careful scrutiny?

Your role. As the consultant, assess whether you are central to or peripheral to the perceived conflict. A central role would be trying to resolve conflicts having to do with your direct interactions with consultees in delivering training, supervision, and intervention recommendations. Sources of conflict beyond your control could be a consultee's dissatisfaction with administration and operations at the educational and treatment setting.

Clarify the issues. Be specific about the conflicts that need to be remedied before continuing with consultation. Present the details to consultees in a group forum and ask for clarification. For example, if consultees have not been implementing an instructional plan with integrity, the consultant might identify that they are uncomfortable with the procedures and seem conflicted about having to continue with the plan as written. The consultant should convey these impressions to the consultees, requesting that they speak forthrightly in order to confirm or disconfirm the source of conflict.

Build consensus. Find areas of agreement among consultees, as depicted in the preceding example, allowing you to begin the process of conflict resolution. Encourage consultees to propose corrective actions. Next, the consultant and consultees should assess the relative strengths-weaknesses of each proposal. The group then selects an alternative that everyone can commit to.

Evaluation. One of the best conflict resolution strategies available to consultants is continuous and objective evaluation. The message to consultees is that the effects of mutually derived solution decisions will be measured empirically according to predetermined outcome criteria. The direction from a consultant should be that performance-based evaluation will be used to confirm successful solutions and to withdraw plans that are ineffective. This approach forms an alliance with consultees—we manage conflicts by systematically evaluating the results of decisions intended to resolve them. *Scope of responsibility.* Conflicts that go beyond a consultant's purview and scope of responsibility will appear with regularity. I have had consultees confide in me about conflicts with employers, how much money they are paid, unsatisfying relationships with coworkers, unpleasant working conditions, and complicated issues in their personal lives. A consultant can listen empathically but should cautiously avoid offering guidance or telling a consultee what to do. This stance towards conflict resolution is similar to the edict of only practicing within one's boundaries of competency. You do not want to tread into territory that is beyond your control, reflects poorly on professional discretion, and could disrupt the consultant—consultee relationships you have formed.

CHAPTER SUMMARY

- Be aware of and consistently demonstrate behaviors that consultees like from consultants.
- Some commonly recognized likeability characteristics are emotional stability, physical appearance, communication style, attentive listening, and dependability.
- Manage performance by focusing on schedule efficiency, preparing to do lists, and arranging productive habits in the office.
- Understand the origins of conflicts that often arise during consultation.
- Confirm your scope of consultation responsibility as a first step towards conflict resolution.

CHAPTER *10*

Technology

Many recent advancements in technology enable consultants to deliver services more effectively (Luiselli & Fischer, 2016). Various technology supports contribute to assessment, data-recording, observations, intervention evaluation, and many facets of consultation, training, and supervision. Like any element of consultation practice, decisions if and how to integrate technology depend on the purpose of such utilization, procedural expertise, and necessary resources. There are also several technology-specific considerations such as systems design, quality of computer and mobile device applications, usage feasibility, and cost of purchasing and updating equipment. Privacy-security precautions further extend to technology-sourced communication modalities.

Minimally, consultants should have facility with electronic correspondence and word-processing software. Being familiar with technology supports for preparing graphs quickly and with precision is another skill integral to behavioral consultation (Dixon, Jackson, Small et al., 2009). To aid with training and supervision, consultants should master rudimentary aspects of graphic design using a program such as *Microsoft PowerPoint*.

Three other technology supports for consultants, reviewed in this chapter, are teleconsultation via videoconferencing, automated data-recording, and video modeling. Table 10.1 is a short list of respective information resources.

TELECONSULTATION

Teleconsultation refers to service delivery using videoconferencing, web-camera observations, distance learning modules, and similar media. Conducting teleconsultation allows consultants to reach consultees in educational and treatment settings that are remote and distant, spending less time on the road and more time devoted to actual practice. A

Conducting Behavioral Consultation in Educational and Treatment Settings.
DOI: https://doi.org/10.1016/B978-0-12-814445-9.00010-9

Table 10.1 Technology Aids and Supports
Videoconferencing
Adobe Connect
CISCO
GoToMeeting
HighFive
Join.Me
Skype
Automated Data-Recording
Behavior Snap
Behavior Tracker Pro
DataFinch
Noldus
SymTrend
Video Modeling
AutisMate 365
iModeling
iMovie
Pinnacle Studio
VideoTote
Visual Impact

second contribution of teleconsultation is enabling consultants to interact simultaneously with several consultees in more than one location. Groups of consultees can also be assembled conveniently at the same time for consultant-delivered training sessions and topical presentations. With regard to observations, events can be documented in real time, recorded for later review, including low frequency but clinically relevant behaviors that might not occur when a consultant is present.

Videoconferencing is perhaps the most readily available method of teleconsultation. Fischer, Clark, Askings, and Lehman (2017) thoroughly reviewed contemporary videoconference options and presented implementation guidelines:

1. Notably, consultants must be familiar with and adhere to the security features of computers and mobile devices. Educational and treatment centers receiving consultation services must be similarly informed. These safeguards include but are not limited to ensuring

confidentiality of communications, having access to audio–video muting, managing video recording, and controlling the number of viewing sessions open at a single time. Ensure that the technology you are using is HIPPA and FERPA compliant.

2. Educational and treatment settings need to be fully equipped with quality up-to-date devices to support videoconferencing as a component of teleconsultation. Poorly configured equipment-devices and problems with connectivity will hamper the efficiency of conference transmission.

3. Be sure that consultees have been trained to use videoconferencing software, there is technology support available, and guidelines are in place for correcting transmission failures.

4. Not every educational and treatment setting will be prepared to receive consultation services via videoconferencing. A setting's responsiveness and receptivity will be determined by prior experiences with the technology, availability of laptop, platform, and web-camera devices, allowable budgets to purchase and maintain equipment, resource sophistication, and privacy-security concerns. Notwithstanding the practical benefits, a consultant may decide that videoconferencing is too labor and resource intensive for some settings.

5. Make the format of videoconferencing sessions identical to face-to-face meetings: prepare and distribute an agenda, be clear about session start-stop times, document attendance, allocate discussion to each agenda item, and record session notes.

6. Some consultees may not want to participate in or be recorded during videoconferencing sessions. Appropriate consents describing videoconferencing procedures, session participants, and viewing protocol should be obtained.

7. Videoconferencing, like other technology applications and methods of teleconsultation, is a tool that may or may not enhance service delivery. Consultants should weigh the pros and cons of videoconferencing against the many practical, ethical, and implementation prerequisites that govern success.

AUTOMATED DATA-RECORDING

During and following observations, consultants usually record data, summarize the results, and construct tables and graphs. As noted, consultants also train consultees to record data while implementing intervention plans and systems projects. For some time, behavior analysts have relied on pencil-and-paper recording, entering data on customized forms contained on clipboards and in program binders, the data then converted to hardcopy summary sheets and figures. More recently, computer-assisted data-recording and summarization have become popular and for several reasons has appeal for consultants.

Portability, ease of input, and integrated systems are strengths of automated data-recording using smart phones, laptops, and tablet devices. The data technologies and applications listed in Table 10.1 are just a few examples among an ever-growing and sophisticated number of choices. These and other tools enable observers to record multiple behaviors, vary measurement methods (frequency, duration, interval), document behavior-specific antecedent–consequence events, and program time-cues and signals. Some other valuable features are rapid conversion of raw data to graphic displays, entering progress notes, and sending information via email.

Research suggests that there may be some advantages of computer-assisted data-recording over traditional pencil-and-paper methods. For consultants, the noteworthy contributions to practice are reduced time, effort, and complexity of conducting and summarizing observations. Most current applications are multifunctional, and highly adaptable, although some have unique system specifications (e.g., Apple, Windows, Android). The proliferation of automated data-recording software and applications will require that consultants diligently scrutinize which products aid service delivery. The related expenses of purchasing and upgrading these tools is another consideration when balancing the advantages and disadvantages of automation. One common mistake is to adopt a new data collection or practice management application simply for the sake of doing so. If you choose to adopt any new piece of technology, make sure to determine the particular problems that it is intended to solve and measure whether it actually produces an improvement in those areas for you.

VIDEO MODELING

Video modeling (VM) lets consultants use technology for intervention and training purposes. Videos are created so that children, adults, and consultees can view models demonstrating responses, behaviors, and entire skills sequences that are consultation objectives. For example, a child or adult receiving self-care training might watch video segments of a model performing routines correctly before receiving instruction from a consultee. Other targets addressed through VM include communication, social, play, daily living, vocational, and leisure skills. Videos can be created with surrogate, actual, and self models. Television monitors, computers, iPads, DVD players, and smart phones offer video viewing in a format that can be individualized to each person's preferences.

Training consultees through VM facilitates consultation in many ways. Consultee performance goals such as implementing DTT, different prompting procedures, behavior support plans, and physical management can be trained with skilled video depictions and later supervised practice. These videos can be standardized and focus on consultee competencies that are finely tuned to performance expectations. Training may be further enhanced by integrating voice-over narration, stop-action, and highlighting features within videos. Individual consultee or group viewing can be arranged with a consultant present or separately to accommodate scheduling restrictions. Multiple viewings by consultees gives them more intensive training opportunities than would be available through consultant-delivered live sessions.

As more and more educational and treatment settings embrace technology, consultants may find that VM is one of the easiest applications to integrate with routine practice. Again, the cost of materials and devices, setting resources, and procedural expertise have to be taken into account. However, the greater affordability and simplicity of installing, running, and maintaining commercial products suggests increased utilization of VM by consultants.

CHAPTER SUMMARY

- Consultants can integrate many technology advancements to improve and enhance service delivery.
- Videoconferencing, automated data-recording, and VM are three technology-delivered methods.
- Use of technology in consultation depends on efficiency and effectiveness, responsiveness of consultees, service setting resources,

implementation expertise, materials-equipment costs, and adherence of security-privacy safeguards.
- Technology systems and applications change rapidly—carefully review quality, adaptability, training, and maintenance specifications.

CHAPTER *11*

Summary and Final Thoughts

Behavioral consulting is not for every human services and behavioral health-care professional. In this guidebook, I have tried to show that having knowledge of learning principles, theory, and the research literature will only go so far if a consultant has poor communication and interpersonal skills. And yet, a socially sophisticated and persuasive consultant will not succeed without technical expertise. Add to the mix that consultants who lack performance management abilities will be ineffective despite their knowledge and practice competencies. I hope my message has been clear that functioning optimally as a consultant is a multifaceted endeavor built on a solid foundation of academic learning, supervised field training, mentoring, extensive experience, continuing education, and relentless self-evaluation.

This concluding chapter briefly summarizes what I consider the best predictors of peak performance in delivering consultation services, a kind of "top-ten" list I have gleaned from many years of practice and observation.

1. Stay within your competency boundaries, acknowledge what you do not know, and educate yourself about unfamiliar areas that impact consultation practice.
2. Be aware that consultees are always forming opinions about you. Act with humility, deference to individual differences, a "can do" attitude, and receptivity.
3. Understand the motivations of consultees when framing consultation advice and recommendations. What do they want from you and can you deliver?
4. Study how to operate functionally in settings where you are not in control and you have to abandon a self-perceived role as expert.
5. Continuously assess your consultation competencies, effectiveness, acceptability, and limitations.
6. Behave in the interest of consultees and not to advance your self-worth and personalized image.

Conducting Behavioral Consultation in Educational and Treatment Settings.
DOI: https://doi.org/10.1016/B978-0-12-814445-9.00011-0

7. Pragmatics are the rule: do what you say, be dependable, manage performance, and pay attention to the details.
8. Gear your verbal and written communications to the aptitudes and receptivity of consultees.
9. Familiarize yourself with and scrupulously follow ethical codes of conduct of your licensing-credentialing boards.
10. Set professional performance goals you want to achieve and form a career development plan.

Flexibility is another strong contributor to consultation success, as conveyed in preceding chapters about scheduling, conducting meetings, delivering supervision, resolving disputes, addressing training needs, and myriad other performance demands. Consistency of work habits is necessary but being able to adjust and revise preferred plans is equally important in the world of consultation. There will be canceled meetings, schedule changes, personnel shifts, unexpected administrative decisions, and similar occurrences in a long list of events that require flexibility of thoughts and actions. Such situations, most of them beyond a consultant's control, can be interpreted as a test of one's resolve to engage in purposeful problem-solving with consultees. I also suggest that you take a look at the current state of mindfulness and mindfulness-based applications for personal growth, something that several prominent, highly regarded, and widely published behavioral professionals have advanced convincingly (Hayes, Strosahl, & Wilson, 2016; Singh, 2014). Mindfulness practices instruct in-the-moment attention, absent judgmental thinking, with acceptance, and positive regard for fluctuating circumstances. In my analysis, being truly mindful defines flexibility.

My emphasis on performance management on the job does not exclude life away from the job. Many professionals, including consultants, disregard the work–life balance to the point that their performance actually suffers. There are always consultation tasks and activities to be completed at home, in the evenings, and on weekends, but without careful diligence the work can become all-encompassing. The starting point for striking a work–life balance is recognizing when the distinction between behavior on the job and away from the job becomes blurred and needs fixing. A few tips in this guidebook may help and in consequence, allow you to consult more efficiently and effectively. Practicing good performance management tactics should enable you to get more work accomplished in less time, reducing tasks and activities to be done at home. Attention to personal health and wellness is vital to peak performance, namely eating nutritious foods, exercising regularly, eliminating consummatory risk factors, and finding calming routines such as mediation, yoga, and simple periods of contemplative silence. Nurturing your caring relationships with spouses, partners, children, relatives, and friends is also performance-enhancing.

Finally, consultants should actively engage in dissemination activities. Consultation performed in educational and treatment settings is at the heart of real-world practice. Through dissemination, you present empirically and socially validated practices to the professional community, students, trainees, and lay public. Consultants can approach dissemination by offering training seminars that teach contemporary approaches to supporting children and adults in educational and treatment settings. A second dissemination target is making presentations at local, regional, and national conferences. Most conferences have ample presentation formats such as symposia, workshops, panel discussions, and poster sessions, allowing consultants to make their work visible to wide audiences. I strongly recommend that consultants write for publication as not only another dissemination activity but also an enriching avenue towards professional development. Organizational periodicals, practice newsletters, journal articles, book reviews, and online forums are just some of the worthy publication outlets. Several sources are available that describe many steps consultants can follow to achieve these dissemination objectives (Friman, 2017; Kelley et al., 2015; Luiselli, 2010, 2017).

BIBLIOGRAPHY

Austin, J. (2000). Performance analysis and performance diagnostics. In J. Austin, & J. E. Carr (Eds.), *Handbook of applied behavior analysis* (pp. 321–349). Reno, NV: Context Press.

Bailey, J. S., & Burch, M. R. (2016). *Ethics for behavior analysts* (3rd ed.). New York: Routledge.

Barlow, D. H., Nock, M. K., & Hersen, M. (2009). *Single-case experimental designs: Strategies for studying behavior change* (3rd ed.). Boston, MA: Allyn & Bacon.

Behavior Analyst Certification Board. (2017). *Professional and ethical compliance code for behavior analysts.* Littleton, CO: Behavior Analyst Certification Board.

Brodhead, M. T. (2015). Maintaining professional relationships in an interdisciplinary setting: Strategies for navigating nonbehavioral treatment recommendations for individuals with autism. *Behavior Analysis in Practice, 8,* 70–78.

Call, N. A., Scheithauer, M. C., & Mevers, J. L. (2017). Functional behavioral assessments. In J. K. Luiselli (Ed.), *Applied behavior analysis advanced guidebook: A manual for professional practice* (pp. 41–72). New York: Academic Press.

Carr, J. E., Wilder, D. A., Majdalany, L., Mathisen, D., & Strain, L. A. (2013). An assessment-based solution to a human-service employee performance problem: An initial evaluation of the *Performance Diagnostic Checklist—Human Services. Behavior Analysis in Practice, 6,* 16–32.

DiGennaro Reed, F. D., & Jenkins, S. R. (2013). Consultation in public school settings. In D. D. Reed, F. D. DiGennaro Reed, & J. K. Luiselli (Eds.), *Handbook of crisis intervention and developmental disabilities* (pp. 317–330). New York: Springer.

Dixon, M. R., Jackson, J. W., Small, S. L., Horner-King, M. J., Lik, N. M. K., Garcia, Y., ... Rosales, R. (2009). Creating single-subject design graphs in Microsoft Excel™ 2007. *Journal of Applied Behavior Analysis, 42,* 277–293.

Durand, V. M. (2008). *When children don't sleep well: Interventions for pediatric sleep disorders.* New York: Oxford University Press.

Durand, V. M., & Crimmins, D. B. (1988). Identifying the variables maintaining self-injurious behavior. *Journal of Autism and Developmental Disorders, 18,* 99–117.

D'Zurilla, T. J., & Goldfried, M. R. (1971). Problem solving and behavior modification. *Journal of Abnormal Psychology, 78,* 107–126.

Erchul, W. P., & Martens, B. K. (2010). *School consultation: Conceptual and empirical bases of practice* (3rd ed.). New York: Springer.

Fischer, A. J., Clark, R., Askings, D., & Lehman, E. (2017). Technology and telehealth applications. In J. K. Luiselli (Ed.), *Applied behavior analysis advanced guidebook: A manual for professional practice* (pp. 135–163). New York: Academic Press.

Fong, E. H., Catagnus, R. M., Brodhead, M. T., Quigley, S., & Field, S. (2016). Developing cultural awareness skills of behavior analysts. *Behavior Analysis in Practice, 9,* 84–94.

Friman, P. C. (2017). Practice dissemination: Public speaking. In J. K. Luiselli (Ed.), *Applied behavior analysis advanced guidebook: A manual for professional practice* (pp. 349–365). New York: Academic Press.

Gilligan, K. T., Luiselli, J. K., & Pace, G. M. (2007). Training paraprofessional staff to implement discrete trial instruction: Evaluation of a practical performance feedback intervention. *The Behavior Therapist, 30,* 63–66.

Gutkin, T. B., & Curtis, M. J. (1982). School-based consultation: Theory and techniques. In C. R. Reynolds, & T. B. Gutkin (Eds.), *The handbook of school psychology* (pp. 796–828). New York: Wiley.

Hayes, S. C., Strosahl, K. D., & Wilson, K. G. (2016). *Acceptance and commitment therapy: The process and practice of mindful change* (2nd ed.). New York: Guilford.

Iwata, B. A., DeLeon, I. G., & Roscoe, E. M. (2013). Reliability and validity of the functional analysis screening tool. *Journal of Applied Behavior Analysis, 46*, 271–284.

Kazdin, A. E. (1977). Assessing the clinical or applied importance of behavior change through social validation. *Behavior Modification, 1*, 427–452.

Kazdin, A. E. (2011). *Single-case research designs: Methods for clinical and applied settings* (2nd ed.). New York: Oxford University Press.

Kelley, D. P., Wilder, D. A., Carr, J. E., Rey, C., Green, N., & Lipschultz, J. (2015). Research productivity among practitioners in behavior analysis: Recommendations from the prolific. *Behavior Analysis in Practice, 8*, 201–206.

Kratochwill, T. R., & Bergan, J. R. (1990). *Behavioral consultation in applied settings: An individual guide.* New York: Plenum Press.

Kratochwill, T. R., Eliot, S. N., & Stoiber, K. C. (2002). Best practices in school-based problem-solving consultation. In A. Thomas, & J. Grimes (Eds.), *Best practices in school psychology-IV* (pp. 583–608). Bethesda, MD: National Association of School Psychology.

Lindsley, O. R. (1991). From technical jargon to plain English for application. *Journal of Applied Behavior Analysis, 24*, 449–458.

Luiselli, J. K. (1998). Maintenance of behavioral interventions. *Mental Health Aspects of Developmental Disabilities, 1*, 69–76.

Luiselli, J. K. (2009). Effects of a performance management intervention on frequency of behavioral supervision at a specialized school for students with developmental disabilities. *Journal of Developmental and Physical Disabilities, 20*, 53–61.

Luiselli, J. K. (2010). Writing for publication: A performance enhancement guide for the human services professional. *Behavior Modification, 34*, 459–473.

Luiselli, J. K. (2013). Descriptive analysis of a staff injury-reduction intervention in a human services setting for children and youth with intellectual and developmental disabilities. *Behavior Modification, 37*, 665–679.

Luiselli, J. K. (2017). Practice dissemination: Writing for publication. In J. K. Luiselli (Ed.), *Applied behavior analysis advanced guidebook: A manual for professional practice* (pp. 325–347). New York: Academic Press.

Luiselli, J. K., & Diament, C. (Eds.), (2002). *Behavior psychology in the schools: Innovations in evaluation, support, and consultation.* West Hazleton, PA: The Haworth Press.

Luiselli, J. K., & Fischer, A. J. (Eds.), (2016). *Computer-assisted and web-based innovations in psychology, special education, and health.* New York: Academic Press.

Mattson, G. G. (2017). Continuing education: Accessing the peer-reviewed literature. In J. K. Luiselli (Ed.), *Applied behavior analysis advanced guidebook: A manual for professional practice* (pp. 309–324). New York: Academic Press.

Neidert, P. L., Rooker, G. W., Bayles, M. W., & Miller, J. R. (2013). Functional analysis of problem behavior. In D. D. Reed, F. D. DiGennaro Reed, & J. K. Luiselli (Eds.), *Handbook of crisis intervention and developmental disabilities* (pp. 147–167). New York: Springer.

Paclawskyj, T. R., Matson, J. L., Rush, K. S., Smalls, Y., & Vollmer, T. R. (2000). Questions about behavior function (QABF): A behavioral checklist for functional assessment of aberrant behavior. *Research in Developmental Disabilities, 21*, 223–229.

Parsons, M. B., & Reid, D. H. (2011). Reading groups: A practical means of enhancing professional knowledge among human service practitioners. *Behavior Analysis in Practice, 4*, 53.

Parsons, M. B., Rollyson, J. H., & Reid, D. H. (2013). Teaching practitioners to conduct behavioral skills training: A pyramidal approach for training multiple human service staff. *Behavior Analysis in Practice, 6*, 4−16.

Schmidt, J. S., Urban, K. D., Luiselli, J. K., White, C., & Harrington, C. (2013). Improving appearance, organization, and safety of special education classrooms: Effects of staff training in a human services setting. *Education and Treatment of Children, 36*, 1−13.

Sellers, T. P., Alai-Rosales, S., & MacDonald, R. P. F. (2016). Taking full responsibility: The ethics off supervision in behavior analytic practice. *Behavior Analysis in Practice, 9*, 299−308.

Sellers, T. P., Valentino, A. L., & LeBlanc, L. A. (2016). Recommended practices for individual supervision of aspiring behavior analysts. *Behavior Analysis in Practice, 9*, 274−286.

Singh, N. N. (2014). *Psychology of mediation*. New York: Nova Science.

Turner, L. B. (2017). Behavior analytic supervision. In J. K. Luiselli (Ed.), *Applied behavior analysis advanced guidebook: A manual for professional practice* (pp. 3−20). New York: Academic Press.

Turner, L. B., Fischer, A. J., & Luiselli, J. K. (2016). Towards a competency-based, ethical, and socially valid approach to the supervision of applied behavior analytic trainees. *Behavior Analysis in Practice, 9*, 287−298.

Valentino, A. L., Sellers, T. P., & LeBlanc, L. A. (2016). The benefits of group supervision and a recommended structure for implementation. *Behavior Analysis in Practice, 9*, 320−328.

Wolf, M. M. (1978). Social validity: The case for subjective measurement or hoe applied behavior analysis is finding its heart. *Journal of Applied Behavior Analysis, 11*, 203−214.

INDEX

Note: Page numbers followed by "*f*" and "*t*" refer to figures and tables, respectively.

CPI Antony Rowe
Chippenham, UK
2019-02-11 11:52